Chillin

A Handbook of American Street Gangs

H. Lynn Russell, Ph.D.

WARNING

The following pages contain material some may find objectionable. A valuable discussion of gangs requires the inclusion of information covering all gang activity. This includes descriptions of the often violent and demeaning behavior most gangs perpetrate. We apologize if this is offensive to you.

How to use this handbook

The information contained in these pages is the result of a lifetime of experience. Some outside sources were used but the majority of information has been compiled first-hand. An outline format and bullet points were used to make it easy to locate information and grasp it quickly. If you would like to view additional information including color photos not in this handbook, we suggest you visit the Gangstopper website at *www.gangstopper.com*

High Hopes Publishing
a subsidiary of
Communication Arts Multimedia, Inc.
Pennsylvania and Texas

For information contact High Hopes Publishing, 226 Scenic View Lane, Ligonier, PA 15658. Attention editors: Pamela Horton, Ph.D. and Eugene Vasconi. 1-888-742-0074

Library of Congress Control Number: 2007922908

ISBN: 978-0-9708417-4-2

First printing: 2007

About H. Lynn Russell, Ph.D.

Dr. H. Lynn Russell is a dynamic public school administrator with half a century of diverse, exciting, and uniquely successful public school experience. He specialized in transforming schools and programs with problems into schools and programs with pride.

Education:

1969 Ph.D., The University of Texas at Austin
1962 M.Ed., Northwestern State University, Louisiana
1958 B.S., Northwestern State University, Louisiana
Dr. Russell has been a college teacher, a regional field service agent, director of a statewide violence prevention program, a central office administrator, and a state assistant commissioner of education. He also served as the principal of small rural schools and large urban campuses in elementary, middle, and high schools, including twelve years at the largest high school in Central Texas. He is currently the Gang Prevention Specialist for Educational Service Center Region 12 in Waco, Texas.

His career of more than forty years spanned the eras of school integration, school riots, student walkouts and sit-ins, and the entrance of drugs, gangs, cults, and deadly violence into the American educational arena. The wealth of information contained in this handbook is the result of intense, personal interactions with gang members and a dedication to understanding this phenomenon.

Dr. Russell's speaking presentations are drawn from real, hands-on experiences with gangs and other violent situations on school campuses. His engagements vary from hour-long keynote addresses to in-depth training workshops. You may contact him through the Gangstopper web site at *mail@gangstopper.com* or through High Hopes Publishing at 1-888-742-0074

This handbook is dedicated with great respect and admiration to:

The Badge: Lieutenant Stan Simpson and
                  Sergeant Rod Hampton
                  Round Rock Police Department
                  Round Rock, Texas

The Bar: Judge Ken Anderson
                  277th District Court
                  Williamson County, Texas
                  (Former District Attorney
                  Williamson County, Texas)

The Bench: Congressman John R. Carter
                  U. S. House of Representatives, District # 31
                  (Former Judge, 277th District Court Texas)

The Book: David Carlin, Deputy Principal
                  Round Rock High School

And Several Friends:

                  Keith Hickman and his staff at Keith A. Hickman
                  Architects and Planners, and
                  Dr. Tom Norris, Executive Director of Region 12
                  Education Service Center and his wonderful staff,
                  for years of support and encouragement.

Acknowledgements:

To my editors and long-time friends…

Except for the faith Pamela Horton, Ph.D. and Gene Vasconi had in me, and their unfailing willingness to pull, push, prod, and poke me into meeting deadlines, this book would not have been completed.

Table Of Contents

"2 get jumped n i had 2 do a six penny pickup 2 save larry which means i had 2 fight 4 gees off for 60 seconds while i tride 2 pick up six pennies they dropped on tha ground n they whipped my ass good but i fought they back hard as i could n tore out Otesses ear ring n messed Tray face all up n got tha other 2 bad but i didn't fall down n i got they respect n tha jefe told them to stop n all shook my hand n hugged me n i felt loved."

1. Introduction

Prior to the 1960s, most Americans knew that street gangs existed but considered them to be merely groups of people in large cities who associated on the streets, somewhat like comedic "Our Gang" and the "Bowery Boys" as presented in the black and white movie shorts and early television.

However, criminal gangs are not a recent American phenomenon, and there is nothing amusing about their origins, growth, and vicious activities.

One of the first recorded instances of criminal street gang activity can be found in 2 Kings 2:23-25 of the Holy Bible, which tells the story of a group of young thugs who emerged from the city and taunted and harassed the prophet Elisha.

Not one to be hampered by legal technicalities, Elisha dealt handily and harshly with the young toughs. He called from Heaven a curse in the form of two she bears, that killed forty-two of the youthful gang members.

In another early record in 1200 AD, a vicious criminal gang called the Thuggi pillaged and murdered throughout India. They had their own secret symbols, ceremonies, hand signs and slang. They were so vicious that they are remembered to this day, and many modern gang members proudly tattoo the words "thug" or "thug life" across their knuckles.

In the mid-1800's, young people's common knowledge of gang behavior was illustrated by Mark Twain's hero Tom Sawyer, who proposed organizing a secret gang of youths, and even wrote a bloody oath to be taken by recruits.

Throughout the 1800's, Americans seem to have had a fascination with gangs and gangsters. The Jesse James gang achieved fame during those years of the Wild West. During the depression, the Barrow Gang and Bonnie and Clyde became folk heroes.

From America's earliest years, wave after wave of an increasing influx of foreign immigrants poured into the country and settled in crowded urban areas, creating ethnic dissension and increased competition for education, jobs, and a share of the new country's bounty.

Uneducated, facing prejudice at every turn, and unable to find social, cultural, or economic success -- and lacking access to meaningful employment -- many young people found their lives filled with boredom, frustration, hopelessness, and poverty. It is small wonder that many of them ended up on the streets in large numbers, and by the 19th century had formed many adult street gangs that specialized in criminal activity and perpetuated themselves through new recruits.

By the early 1800's, many of the most vicious adult street gangs had organized along ethnic, neighborhood, and political lines. Years of corruption in city government and attendant intensification of urban problems immediately preceding the Civil War contributed to the rapid increase of criminal street gangs formed to protect neighborhoods where these gangs were located.

In New York City, the Smith's Valley gang and the Broadway Boys were all white. Only Blacks were allowed in the Long Bridge Boys and the Fly Boys, and there were a number of notable all-Irish and all-Italian gangs.

Herbert Ashley's 1932 book <u>Gangs of New York</u> was inspired by the 1840-1863 bloody clashes between the "native" and "immigrant" gangs in the squalid Five Points area. The 2002 movie by the same name glamorized the bloody exploits of real-life gang members such as Bill the Butcher, Stumpy Marlarky, Goo-Goo Knox, Piker Ryan, Hoggy Walsh, Johnny Spanish, Monk Eastman, Fig McGerald, Googy Corcoran, Baboon Conally, Big Josh Hines, and Red Rock Farrell.

This movie was the first exposure and education of many modern Americans to any type of criminal gang life. It chronicled the exploits of the vicious street gangs of the mid-1800's, such as the Forty Thieves (first New York gang, all Irish) Chichesters, Roach Guards, Plug Uglies, Shirt Tails (always out), Bowery Boys, Whyos, Daybreak Boys, Swamp Angels, and

Dead Rabbits ("dead rabbit" was street slang for a very rowdy, immensely strong person).

Some aspects of contemporary American gang culture date back to these early gangs, including the use of uniform dress styles, gang colors, symbols, street names, hand signals, and codes.

Following the Civil War, street gangs began to appear throughout the country, and criminal violence and involvement with drugs became permanently linked with the American gang scene. The level of violence, improvements in methods of transportation, and the increased availability of firearms broadened and intensified the scope of gang activity.

The worsening economy of the early 1900s and attendant problems in large cities brought on mass influxes of ever-increasing diverse cultures, and the gap between the U.S. rich and poor widened. In urban areas populated by poor, uneducated, and hopeless people, gangs, gang warfare, and criminal activity thrived along ethnic, cultural, and racial lines.

The ethnic and largely non-white nature of these gangs continued to be determined in great part by the patterns of immigration and migration of various ethnic groups to major cities in the United States. Typical of this influx of new cultures into large American cities, African Americans from the Deep South and Hispanics from Mexico and South America migrated to northern cities by the thousands. Concentrated in the poorer neighborhoods, predominately Black and Latin communities, especially Mexican, gave rise to organized street gangs such as the Latin Kings and Vice Lords in Chicago, New York, and west coast cities of the United States.

Spurred by conditions in Mexico following the Revolution during the 1920's, hundreds of thousands of Mexican citizens found refuge in or near established Hispanic communities in beautiful but sparsely settled area of East Los Angeles they called La Maravilla, from which came the name of the clique of gangs that developed in that area and spread across the rest of East Los Angeles.

In New York, major street gangs such as La Familia, Savage Skulls, Savage Nomads, and the Rampers came to power. By the end of World War II, street gangs were beginning to warrant increasing public concern. They had developed a more rigid, formal organization that included gang colors, signs, and symbols, and were composed mainly of teenagers and young adults who committed major criminal acts, often with firearms. The era of better-organized, extremely violent and often deadly street fights with modern weaponry between and among gangs had begun.

Beyond the sanctity of the home and school, adolescent needs met head-on with the reality of the streets. There, a poor, angry, under-educated minority youth from a dysfunctional family, harboring a multitude of societal ills and little chance of conventional success, could join a gang and become an instant "somebody". Unable to depend upon his biological family for basic needs, often abused and neglected, he found it easier to conduct his life and make his way on the street rather than remain in poverty, violence, and despair in his home. As a new gang member, he had immediate access to a new "family", complete with a sense of belonging, concern, approval, discipline, and protection. The gang family came complete with weapons, cars, money, sex, drugs, parties, and especially with "love" and "respect" -- gangster style.

From the ranks of such disenfranchised youths, gang membership increased daily and gang activity escalated throughout the first half of the 20th century. Decade after decade, generation after generation, younger members were imbued with increasingly formalized gang lore based on intense violence and a twisted, inflexible code of loyalty, turf, honor, revenge, and retaliation. By the early 1960s, gang conflict in major American cities was at an all-time high.

During the 1960s, the escalation of criminal youth gangs was briefly overshadowed by the public's preoccupation with the Vietnam War and the Civil Rights movement. Political scandals and worldwide problems moved gang violence from the front page of American consciousness. During this period, gang violence also dipped slightly due to the numbing effects of increased drug use by gang members, many of whom were often so spaced out that they could not conduct gang activities.

The respite in gang violence was short-lived, and by the late 1960s drug use by gang members had decreased -- some gangs banned drug use by their members -- and drug sales by gangs exploded. Rivalry for control of the criminal drug trade escalated gang violence into open street warfare fought with weapons that outgunned even well equipped police departments.

During the 1970's, the American economy changed from a manufacturing-based to a service-based economy fueled by high tech industry, reducing the demand for low-skilled workers. Many lower socio-economic citizens were driven into a vicious cycle of low paying jobs, temporary positions, and even permanent joblessness with few benefits, if any. To survive, entire generations of families resorted to welfare, assistance from their extended family, or criminal activity.

By the 1980s, organized street gangs had become established in every state, and gang culture had undergone several significant changes. The majority of gang violence was no longer centered on girls, turf, and gang, ethnic, and neighborhood honor. Instead, the gangs focused on financial gain, usually from drugs and other major criminal interests. Gang violence intensified and was often committed with the tactical aspects and precision of expert guerrilla warfare brought to the streets by veterans of decades of military service.

Some large street gangs prospered, grew, and spread throughout the nation and even the world to the point they designated themselves as "nations." Eventually, other gangs began to associate themselves with these larger, better organized gangs and align their activities with those of the "nation" with which they affiliated.

Excellent examples of such affiliations are found in the in the Folk and People Nations of Chicago. Various gangs align themselves with one of the other of these, similar to the manner in which various football teams align themselves with the National Football League. The NFL is not a gang in itself; it is a coalition of teams in a league. Similarly, many gangs align under the Folk Nation, many others align among the People nation. Once aligned, the affiliated gangs consider their enemies or friends to be the same as their chosen "nation."

Major gang alliances, once affiliated, soon were spread throughout state and federal penitentiary systems by incarcerated gang members who sought protection and power by recruiting other prisoners and forming coalitions behind the walls as enemies or allies within their different cultures.

On the streets, alliances among national gangs were for convenience, protection, to defend or appropriate territory, or to expedite mutual drug trade or other criminal activities. On occasion, even deadly enmity between traditional gangs such as the Bloods and Crips were set aside for mutual profiting from criminal activities, and enemy gangs would often cut truces in order to relieve law enforcement pressure.

By the early 1990's, gang migration and proliferation reached the point that twenty-five percent of small communities surveyed reported having gang members enrolled in their schools. This situation has only worsened. Today, gangs exist throughout the nation in hundreds of small towns and communities where quiet lifestyles and overtaxed law enforcement resources are ill equipped to handle gang activities.

These national alliances now boast literally hundreds of gangs, often made up of many individual sets -- individual gangs -- which in some cases total thousands of gang members. Surveys of law enforcement agencies indicate that today there are more than twenty-five thousand individual gangs in the United States, with a total membership of approximately eight hundred thousand. California leads the way with three hundred thousand gang members; Texas follows with ninety thousand. ("National Gang threat Assessment" compiled by the

National Gang Investigator's Association and "Gangs in Texas; An Assessment" by the State Attorney General's Office)

These alliances, culture, and their bitterness have progressed inexorably into the suburban and rural communities of America. Rarely do entire gangs move to new locations as a whole; however, on occasion some have relocated their drug sales and other criminal activities *en masse* to more lucrative financial markets. Usually, gangs spread when individual gang members recruit new members, appropriate turf and establish the gang culture as they relocate residences, visit family or friends, move temporarily to hide from the law or from other gangs, find new markets for their activities, or are relocated by court placement.

Attempting to improve their circumstances in life, parents often strive to move out of urban gang-infested neighborhoods, and often relocate to inexpensive housing, often to subsidized public housing projects. Even elementary children in such families are often already involved with gangs, and the gang culture moves with the family, bringing gang culture, philosophy, and activities into areas previously uninfected.

When new markets open, law enforcement pressure builds, or a gang presence is needed to support local gang activity, gangs sometimes relocate to small communities near large cities. Such sparsely settled communities with inadequate law enforcement, isolated homes, and ready access to interstate highways and nearby large cities are ready-made gang havens. Migration of vicious urban gang to small communities also occurs when small local gangs call upon their friends or relatives for assistance with local turf disputes or to expand into more lucrative criminal activities, usually illegal drug sales. The local gangs are exposed to and adopt urban gang culture and folklore, and eventually are absorbed by the incoming gangs

Whatever the cause of migration, gangs have prospered and grown throughout the nation to the extent that some gang-savvy persons agree wryly that if you want to avoid gangs, don't move to the suburbs or the country – *move to the moon!*

Although some American communities are grappling with the root causes of gang activity, they are in the minority; the majority have no gang prevention and intervention programs. Some communities even elect to ignore the obvious presence of street gangs and their activities.

The following chronicle of the growth and proliferation of several major gangs and supremacist groups serves to illustrate the problem facing America.

Crip Gangs

In 1964, a younger gang called the Avenue Boys controlled the area around Central Avenue in Los Angeles and was used by the Black Panthers for minor crimes. Following in the Avenue Boys footsteps, in 1969 fifteen-year-old Raymond "Truck" Washington and his friend Stanley "Tookie" Williams, organized the Baby Avenues gang. Since most of those who joined this gang were students at Washington High School in South Central Los Angeles, they adopted the school's blue and white colors as the gang's colors. These young boys formed the precursor of what would come to be known as the Crips, one of the nations largest and most violent street gangs.

The name change from the Avenue Boys to the Crips occurred when several Avenue gang members attacked a group of local citizens on their way home from a meeting to discuss forming a community group to battle crime, including gang activity, in the local neighborhoods.   When the police arrived, an Asian American lady described in broken English one of the attackers as a "crip" who walked with a limp and carried a walking cane.   The media, always ready for a new angle, termed the attacking gang members as "Crips", and the name stuck.

Crip members often initiate into the gang by committing a crime in front of gang witnesses. The initiation process is called "locking-In". Female members have the option to commit a crime or become "sexed-In" (have sex with several or all gang members). This is also called "pulling a train."

The Crips use identifiers of the Folk Nation. Early on they adopted the color blue for their clothing to set them apart from other gang members. Within Crip sets, light blue continues to be the dominant color. Gang members wear blue and clear beads or blue and white beads around their neck, and mostly blue jeans and a white shirt. However, other dark colors such as black, brown, and purple may be blended to identify certain Crip sets.

An unspoken manner of identifying themselves as Crips is the practice of "repping". "Repping" is representing or favoring one side of the body. Crips "rep" to the right by standing with one foot forward, holding books in their right hands, wearing a bandana in the right pocket, and otherwise indicating their preference for the right side of their body. To set themselves apart from Bloods who use the terms "Bro" and "Dog" when addressing their members, Crips began using the word "Cuzz". Cuzz is a derivative of "Young Cousin", an affectionate nickname.

Crips are deadly enemies with Bloods, whom they call "Slobs", "Slops", and "Oo-lahs."

Blood Gangs

The term "Young Blood" caught on with youthful embattled American soldiers during the Vietnam conflict. The term resonated with gang members on the streets, particularly in the Los Angeles area during the 1950s. When a rift developed in the

Crip gang, a smaller faction that separated from the gang resorted to new levels of violence towards the larger members of the original gang. A considerable amount of blood was spilled on the street as the smaller group resorted to straight razors to survive. Violence was so prevalent that the media took note and once again gave a gang a name, "Bloods".

Originally, Blood gangs were composed of Black individuals. However, as the original Blood gang grew and prospered, Bloods accepted other ethnicities. Since the 1970s, Blood gangs have increased by the thousands and have organized into the United Blood Nation coalition which is affiliated with the People Nation.

Spilling blood is still a trademark of the United Blood Organization. To gain acceptance to a Blood gang, an individual must "blood-in" by spilling someone's blood, or by having his or her own blood spilled. There are various ways to blood-in such as fights, slashing, assaults against law enforcement personnel, rapes, robberies, or group sex for women who are becoming associated with the gang. But in every case someone's blood must be spilled.

Once an individual has become a member of a Blood gang, "blooding out" is the only method of leaving, either by beating or death. An alternative might be, as a final gang duty, shedding the blood of an enemy designated by the gang.

The blooding ritual has even been given a title … "Bibo" for "Blood in, Blood Out.." When questioned about their gang membership, Bloods claim 100% BIBO … 100% Blood.

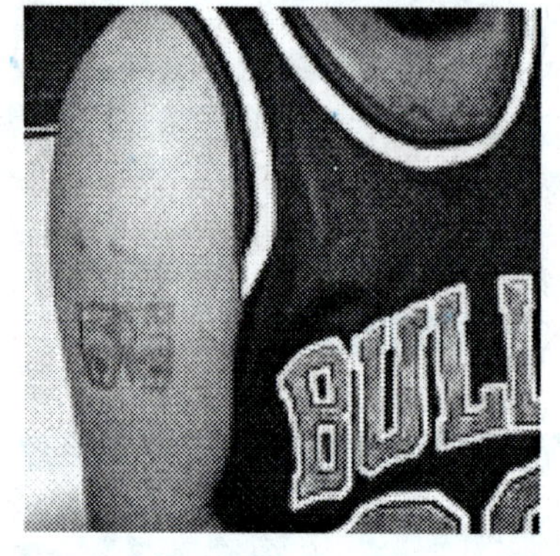

In fact, the spilling of blood has become a common part of the rituals of joining and leaving most, if not all American gangs.

Bloods show their disrespect for Crips by calling them "Scuzz", "E-ricketts", or by the name of any despised clawed creature such as crabs or lice. To compound the insult, Blood tattoos and graffiti often flaunt the word <u>crab</u> upside down or backwards with the "a" replaced by a five-pointed star or crown.

Many Bloods also refuse to use the letter "c" (for Crips), and in writing or speaking will either mark out or change the "c" to a "b". This practice causes some confusion to the uninitiated and unknowing who might hear one Blood tell another, "Pick up that boin on the barpet", or the teacher puzzling over a paper that states, "Baesar bonquered the Bountry." Bloods write in secret codes, some dozens of pages in length, which are changed and/or rewritten regularly to maintain secrecy.

Bloods wear predominately red or red and black clothing often identified with the Chicago Bulls, Blackhawks, or other sports teams with black and red colors. For example, they often wear in their shoes:

- red shoelaces
- two red shoelaces in one shoe and two of another color in the other

- one red shoelace and one other color lace … usually black … in the same shoe.

Other colors are occasionally used if they are significant to the particular gang, such as Lime Street Pirus. The gang's colors range from a bright red to a deep maroon. The brighter the color red worn by a Blood member, the more blood he supposedly has spilled.

Bloods "rep" to their own left. They display gang affiliation by "repping" or accenting to the left in various ways, such as having the left pants leg rolled up, carrying a backpack on the left shoulder, standing with the left foot forward, or with crossed arms having the hand to the left showing and the other hand tucked inside the arm.

Racial Supremacists, Skinheads, and Other Hate Groups

White power, skinheads, neo-nazis, militias, posses and other white racial supremacy groups in the United States number about 300, ranging from religious sects to openly militant and violent neo-Nazi skinhead organizations and Ku Klux Klan Klaverns. These groups thrive on prejudice and fear. The fear they plant is that Blacks, Jews, and non-whites (all termed "mud people") are planning clandestinely to take over all power in the United States and will force whites into deprivation.

To bring attention to their cause and to remind others of their existence, white supremacists often organize their activities and violence to coincide with the anniversaries of significant events or the birthdays of people they admire or hate, such as:

January 8	Birthday of Gordon Kahl (Founder of Posse Comitatus)
January 15	Birthday of Martin Luther King, Jr.
January 16	Birthday of Robert Matthews (Founder of "The Order")
January 30	Adolph Hitler and the Nazi Party take power in Germany 1933)
February 6	Trial of The Order members ends in conviction, 1986
February 18	Aryan Women's League founded in 1989
March 9	Birthday of George Lincoln Rockwell (Founder of the American Nazi Party)
April 4	Assassination of Martin Luther King, Jr. in 1968
April 7	Fort Smith, Arkansas, sedition trial victory in 1968
April 15	Income Tax Deadline Day Anniversary of the end of the siege at Waco, Texas and the Anniversary of the bombing of the Federal Building in Oklahoma City
April 20	Adolph Hitler's Birthday; National Marijuana Day, Columbine High School Shooting
April 26	Birthday of Rudolf Hess, 1884, Nazi Party Official
May 6	Ku Klux Klan Incorporated in 1866
May 19	Birthday of Malcolm X in 1926
June 3	Birthday of Jefferson Davis, President of the Confederate States Date Tom Metzger (White Aryan Resistance -WAR) won congressional primary in San Diego, California Independence Day, celebrated as Revolution Day by white supremacists and neo-Nazi movements Birthday in 1821 of Nathan Bedford Forest, Confederate General and reputed founder of the Ku Klux Klan

	Birthday of Huey Long, assassinated Louisiana governor, former U.S. Senator, potential U.S. presidential candidate, and creator of the "Share the Wealth" political movement of the 1930's.
August 21-22	Anniversary of the siege at Ruby Ridge with Randy Weaver
September 11	Anniversary of World Trade Center disaster
September 22	Founding of The Order
October 11	National "coming out" day for gays and lesbians Tom Metzger (White Aryan Resistance-WAR leader) convicted in Portland, Oregon, 1990
November 9	Berlin Wall torn down
November 9-10	Kristallnacht, (Night of Glass), German Nazi's terrorized Jews in 1938
November 17	British recognize the right of Jews to a homeland in the Balfour Declaration in 1917
December 8	National Martyrs Day, Whidbey Island standoff by Robert J. Mathews, founder of The Order
December 24	Ku Klux Klan founded in 1865

White racial supremacy groups' strong feelings of white ethnicity are reflected in their philosophies of new-Nazism and racism. Generally, such groups are not concerned with turf as are street gangs.

Supremacists and hate groups can be roughly divided into four parts:

Loners tend to be solitary and may or may not belong to local gangs or supremacy groups, but act and are perceived as loners. Loners often are not trusted by even others with similar beliefs and goals. Such individuals often commit criminal acts on their own.

Thrill-seekers, also called "bashers", are often from affluent homes. Thrill-seekers are generally small, loosely organized groups of white youth who commit hate crimes against others, usually homosexuals or minorities.

Stoners are loosely knit youth groups on the fringes of Skinhead organizations, with common interests in drugs, heavy metal music, and sometimes cults, including satanic worship. Stoners participate in random violence in concert with Skinhead groups.

Skinheads are racial supremacy groups that espouse neo-Nazi beliefs. Skinhead gangs took root in England in the 1970s and 1980s, and can be attributed in great part to the influence of the musical group "Skrewdriver" in England plus the skinhead newsletter Blood and Honor.

2. Gangs and the Law

Most if not all states have specific anti-gang laws. For example, the Texas Penal Code, Section 71.01(d) defines a gang as:

> *"… three or more persons having a common identifying sign or symbol or an identifiable leadership who continuously or regularly associate in the commission of criminal activities."*

In addition, the Texas Education Code 37.121(a,b,c,d) states that:

> *"It is illegal for a person to be a member of, to pledge to become a member of, join, or solicit another person to join or pledge to become a member of a public school fraternity, sorority, secret society, or gang.*
>
> *It is also illegal for a person who is not a public school student to solicit another person to attend a meeting of a fraternity, sorority, secret society, or gang, or a meeting at which the person will be*

encouraged to become a member of such an organization.

Since many people tend to characterize any troublesome group of adolescents group as a gang, it is necessary to be able to distinguish between youth groups and gangs when applying this rule to friendship, school, and community groups of young people who are not in gangs.

A key to deciding between negative street gang-related groups and positive youth service groups is a rough rule-of-thumb …if the group perpetuates itself by decision/vote of the members, it would not normally qualify as a school service group.

3. Gang Characteristics

The following section summarizes many gang characteristics into capsules that can be used for identification and understanding.

A Definition of a Gang

A group of people who want to be seen as different from others and as a distinct organized group and:

- Have regular and continuous fellowship.
- Have leadership.
- Have a geographic, economic, or cultural area of operation.
- Have common territory, group name, identifying behavior, vocabulary, signs, colors, and symbols.
- Are individually or collectively engaged in a pattern of anti-social or criminal activity such as:
  Graffiti, vandalism, intimidation, including:
  - Theft, burglary, robbery, break-ins.
  - Car theft and hijacking.
  - Use and sale of drugs and weapons.
  - Assault, murder, rape.
  - A variety of other criminal activities.

Typical Criteria for Being Considered a Gang Associate/Member

- Self-admission and self-identification, overt or covert:
- Claims gang affiliation.
- Judicial finding of gang membership.
- Is identified as a gang member by law enforcement agency through behavior or

physical evidence such as photos and activities and movements, or association with gang members, gathered by community agencies.
- Is identified as a gang member by a reliable informant.
- Is identified by a dependable informant and that identification is corroborated by other independent information.
- Is identified as a gang member by a parent/guardian.
- Name appears on gang documents, hit list, or gang graffiti.
- Wears or displays gang colors, hair styles, jewelry, symbols, or other gang-related items that clearly indicate gang affiliation.
- Has gang-related tattoos.
- Uses gang hand signs and signals.
- Uses gang language that clearly indicates gang affiliation.
- Writes, wears, or displays gang graffiti.
- Uses gang-related tag name or street name.
- Associates with known gang members; frequents a gang area or resides with known gang members.
- Is involved in criminal gang incidents.
- Has been arrested more than once in the company of identified gang members for offenses consistent with gang activity.

- Subject's victims or targets of crime are members of rival gang.

Factors that contribute to the development and spread of gang culture

Several aspects of our ever-changing American culture have contributed significantly not only to the rapid growth of gangs, but also to public awareness of their presence and knowledge of their activities.

- Some youth join gangs of their own free choice for:
    - Excitement
    - Entertainment
    - Recognition
    - Greed

However, most youth join gangs because of:
- Socioeconomic and environmental factors:
    - Lives in gang-infested neighborhood
    - Family member(s) in a gang
    - Family member(s) in prison
    - Confined in juvenile detention facility
- Tradition

Many young people face pressures from all sides that combine into a vicious cycle and cause gang life to be a viable option. Then, (s)he:

- Fails repeatedly in traditional situations
- Detaches from school; drops out soon as possible
- Sees little chance for:
    - meaningful/positive social success
    - academic achievement
    - meaningful employment
- Blames problems on discrimination, prejudice
- Close ties to gang influences
- Lives in a gang-infested neighborhood
- Close friends are gang member
- Close family member(s) served prison time
- One or more close family members in a gang
- Is confined in a juvenile detention facility

SOME MAJOR CAUSES OF GANGS IN AMERICA
Mobility of American culture
Migration
Media
Deterioration of urban areas
Drugs
Availability of weapons
Modern transpiration
Loss of traditional American values
Breakdown of family unit and loss of family values

Source: U.S. Department of Justice

> *"i feel like a fuccing failure, quit my fuccing job n trying not ta take it ta da streetz ta make mah money but im running out of time. ain't nobody wants ta hire me. i ain't got no fuccing transportation shyt so i can't get to a steady job. School got me doing shyt I don't understand n i read n read it n still don't get it so i haven't been doing that shyt then i get in trouble cuz my work ain't done pluz i ain't been coming here like i should be. i feel like ima failing so bad n losing everything that ima going to fucc up n wind up either back in juve again or ima wind up dead. i got no fuccing money no fuccing job no fuccing chance."*

Several aspects of our ever-changing American culture have contributed significantly not only to the rapid growth of gangs, but also to public awareness of their presence and knowledge of their activities.

Gangs tend to be centralized in impoverished areas of large urban cities where factors such as parental neglect, exposure to violence, lack of jobs and educational opportunities, and poverty disrupt, distort, and destroy children's lives. Furthermore, gangs in these areas tend to have more members who are older and more hardened criminals, and therefore are more violent.

To children growing up in desperate and hopeless circumstances and hungering for identity and recognition, gangs present a viable option. There is little in their lives to discourage gang membership. Too many are unable to resist the constant barrage of movies, videos, role models, fashions, and other temptations that glamorize youthful rebellion and the gangster lifestyle.

Some are intimidated into joining gangs under the very real threat of daily beatings if they refuse; others join for protection from other gangs. Among the many who join for acceptance and companionship are young people with physical or learning disabilities who have been painfully shunned by the mainstream of young society. To such young people, the difference in how others -- especially their peers -- perceive and treat them after they become gang members can be a considerable improvement on their previous status in the school and community.

> *"people say Too-Joe is a bad ass all the way thrugh but it weren't like that he n I n two other homies got caught in a bad situation and we did what we had to do thats why Too-Joe is doing life cause he didn't sell me out we was just paying them back when the Five-O rolled up back n when I hear these ideots I get so angrey they don't know Too-Joe took the fall for all of us n he is a real hero to us on the streets."*

In some families, gang membership is a tradition, an integral part of their family and neighborhood life passed down by their fathers, uncles, and brothers.

New gang members are encouraged by the immediate rewards of illegal gang activities to further themselves in the gang by committing even more serious crimes. In fact, the younger gang members are often assigned the most serious and violent gang crimes, since if caught they will be treated more leniently by the juvenile courts.

Most gang members are not concerned with the implications of their illegal actions; they live in the present and have no goals or future plans beyond the scope of their gang's activities. Additionally, their criminal behavior and defiance of parents, teachers, and society as a whole earn them the approval and respect of their delinquent peers. In the gang they find the success that they could not experience in school.

Gang members expect to go to the hospital, to jail, or to the cemetery. Many of them maintain that the three dots on the web of one hand indicate their realization that gang life will lead them only to one of those three places. Going to prison is to a gang member much like going off to college is for a high

school graduate. Just as the graduate's family and friends hold a party for him, the gang member's family and friends hold a party for the one returning from prison. He has paid his dues; he is now an O.G. ... an Original Gangster ... and has earned "juice" – reputation and respect on the streets.

How They Become Recruits

CHANGES IN MAJOR INFLUENCES ON AMERICAN TEENAGERS	
1950 -1960	1990 – 2000
1. Family	1. Media
2. Church	2. Peers
3. School	3. Family
4. Peers	4. School
5. Media	5. Church

Source: varied plus personal observations

Common Needs of Adolescents

- Affiliation with a group
- A sense of belonging
- Emotional ties
- Family
- Friends
- Protection
- Self-esteem and esteem of their peers
- Status
- An audience for deeds of bravado
- Excitement
- Entertainment
- A sense of future

Results of Adolescent and Pre-Adolescent Neglect and/or Alienation

- Little or no adult supervision
- Little positive guidance
- Few or no positive role models
- Freedom to roam the streets
- Bored, feels inadequate, disenfranchised

- Blames problems on discrimination
- Detached from school, drop out as quickly as possible
- Little identification with school
- Little chance for social or academic success
- Few opportunities for meaningful employment, advancement
- Ready availability of gangs, weapons, and drugs
- Life filled with problems, pain, anger, anguish

What Gangs Claim to Offer Young People

- All of the "Common Needs" above
- A family and many things a family should give a young person, including:
    - Belonging
    - Identity
    - Emotional ties not provided by the family
    - Discipline
    - Love
    - Protection
    - Education
    - Excitement
    - A chance to be somebody,
    - Freedom from traditional family and restrictions
    - Upward mobility - criminal style - something of an immediate future
    - Immediate access to weapons, cars, money, alcohol, drugs, partying, and sex
    - Ethnic identity (sometimes)
    - Admission to a secret group, with secret signs, language, codes, signals, dress, traditions, territory

- A stage for posturing and strutting; applause from an approving audience
- Release from reality, from dysfunctional family, from having to deal with real life problems.
- Fear from other people (which they call "respect")
- And, most appealing, an adolescent's dream -- a culture in which youths are in charge and adults are afraid of them

4. Misjudging Gang Presence

> *"I visited my cousin n Houston his set was called LTO for Latins Taking Over they kick it with this gang called EME there are gangs all over like no matter what hood u go to you know or like what part of the country u visit even in that rich neighborhoodz they be killing each other there is one Crip gang like in one of the rich neighboohods it is a bad muthaf--king set you know you wouldn't think a bunch of rich boyz could f--k up a real bk you know the five o bagged me up and while I was in I kicked it with one of them you know rich boyzs n I thought the Sur or Norte and kick his rich lil boy azz but he wasn't no punk bitch you know he was one mean billy bad ass and got his hustle on and beat the f--king shyt out of one of them and after that everybody gave him his props and he go tthe respect he deservedt."*

It is generally acknowledged that gang members come from all walks of society and can exist in any community. Even so, some "good" parents from "good" homes in "good" neighborhoods still refuse to believe that gang members live in their midst. Whatever their reasons, they continue to ignore the facts that that gangs are caused by something other than run-down neighborhoods, dysfunctional families, and poverty, and that gang philosophy and activities can appeal to "good" children from more affluent families if the factors that contribute to the development and spread of gang culture listed elsewhere in this handbook are met.

The crimes of affluent gangs often will include random violence, and their crimes will be more sophisticated and their methods of gang identification more subtle than those of the usual street gangs.

Media

The media industry and many media personalities, especially rap and sports stars, glorify gangs and their activities by claiming and flaunting former, current, and even imagined gang membership. The media constantly bombards fascinated and impressionable young people with a host of "cool" anti-establishment messages -- replete with vulgarities -- that urge them to "kill cops, f---k hoes and bitches, get high on drugs", and commit other criminal acts.

Seen, heard, or read daily by millions of American youth, these movies, TV shows, videos, and magazines offer powerful anti-social images that entice and teach the gang rhetoric, symbols,

clothes, and activities. It is no longer necessary for youth to be directly in the company of gang members in order to learn and imitate the gangster culture -- they merely have to turn on the television, go to the movies, or read magazines or books that glorify gang activity

Street rap has turned into gangster rap, filled with hate, sex, and anger and glorifying the gangster life, murder, racism and the gangster (usually the rapper himself) in the most obscene and explicit terms and boasts of violence against the establishment.

Fashion

On the fashion scene, fads that were previously promoted by affluent society have given way to ghetto styles to the point that today many originate on the street and are then adopted by the upper classes. Many of today's hottest fads in young people's clothing wear are derived directly from gang culture on the streets. The gangster look is considered to be chic and appeals to teenagers trying to dress to impress other teenages, as well as being offensive to parents, teachers, and others in authority.

5. Street Culture and Lower Socioeconomic Impact

A quick scan of the culture of the streets reveals the odds against today's young people breaking out of the chains of the lower socio-economic status of their lives.

Families

- Low socio-economic status; extreme economic deprivation
- Disorganized, beset with family management problems
- Troubled by such factors as incest, alcohol and drug abuse
- Domestic violence
- Family history of gang involvement
- Broken homes, lack of parental role models, particularly adult male

Parents

- Unskilled, unemployed, or have low incomes; caught in poverty cycle
- Single-parent households or unmarried teen parents
- See little value in appropriate socialization and education
- Use alcohol, illegal drugs
- High incidence of child neglect
- Few parenting skills
- View themselves and their children as victims
- Are dysfunctional persons
- Are negative role models

Self and Peers

- Delinquent in school and community
- In trouble with police
- Low attachment to school and teachers
- Learning disabilities
- Low grades, low test scores
- Street wise
- Defiant
- Deviant attitudes and behavior
- Fatalistic attitude
- Social disabilities; lack refusal skills
- Early or precocious sexual activity
- Problem behaviors,
- Anti-social, aggressive, hostile
- Aggressive
- Victims of abuse and neglect
- Gang association
- Use drugs, alcohol; high availability of weapons, particularly guns
- Feel victimized
- View violence as norm for defense, settling disputes, gaining status

Communities

- High crime rate
- Undergoing changes (racial, income, industrial, rural)
- High unemployment
- High mobility
- Little or no working relationship among local social agencies
- Gangs have staked out turf
- Graffiti and territorial marking
- Assaults and intimidation are frequent
- Area is dirty, rundown, neglected

- Gang activity and crime have existed for a long period of time
- Neighborhood norms support gang activity
- School and area receive bad publicity
- Little opportunity for meaningful work for youths
- Inhabitants feel discriminated against
- Firearms, drugs, alcohol easily available

Schools

- High truancy (partly because students are afraid to travel to school)
- Gang problems in elementary and middle schools
- Low student performance and attendance; high dropout rate
- Low parent involvement
- Teachers have no special training to deal with gangs or social problems
- School personnel have low educational expectations of students
- Students negatively labeled by teachers
- Schools achieve few honors
- Presence of many student problems on campus
- Little participation in school activities
- Few teacher role models

Role models

- American culture has changed its view of role models
- Today's heroes are often sports stars who flaunt alleged gang affiliation and receive perfunctory slaps on the hands for such felony offenses as drugs and assault
- To at-risk children in the ghetto, the pimp is often the epitome of success

Other encouragements to gang formation
- Entertainment industry, media, business culture
- MTV
- Rap music, "gangsta" music
- Clothing
- Many hardcore gangs have adopted designer labels or insignias of sports teams, so there is a crossover between sports fan and gang attire:
  - Back to school sales gimmicks promote not the importance of school, but the fun of buying clothes … often gang clothes
  - Gang attire is displayed with fanfare in stores; even some of the most expensive designers feature it
  - Special "Homie" brand of clothing
  - Clothing often designed with symbols on left or right, according to gangs" left/right orientation

6. The Gang Culture and the Community

A kid growing up in the lower socio-economic strata of society has three strikes against him before he ever steps out of the street where gang traditions are so ingrained in the community that they help perpetuate the gang lifestyle. His own community provides:

- A protected stronghold for gangs.
- Family connections with gangsters.
- A recruitment pool for new gang members
- Important information (police patrols, activities of other possibility of targets for criminal activities)
- Protection for cultural groups in certain communities and are viewed by some as the only protection they have against criminal enterprise.

How many young people belong to gangs?

- Ten to twelve percent of young people in poverty neighborhoods may be involved with gangs as some stage of gang involvement, such as:
  - Fantasy
  - Wannabes - also known by police as "gonnnabes"
  - Affiliates
  - Members
  - Hardcore criminals
- Most enter gang activity during 7th and 8th grade.
- Some grow up in gangs from their youngest years.
- There are approximately as many street gangs in America as there are Wendy's, McDonald's, and Burger King restaurants combined – approximately twenty-five thousand.

Composition of the membership of the estimated 28,000 gangs in America

Source: Department of Justice National Youth Gang Survey

Average age	15.9 yrs
14 years old or younger	11%
15 - 17 years old	29%
18 - 26 years old	46%
Male	92%
Black	48%
Hispanic	43%
White	5%
Asian	4%
Below average grade level	70%
Fulltime students with poor attendance	70%
Removed from school while juveniles	13%
More than one felony arrest	64%
Have committed crimes against persons	57%
Live with both parents	23%

- On welfare, disability, social security   55%
- Family income below $1000/month   61%
- Three or more siblings under 18   50%
- Have siblings who have been arrested   36%
- Are in some special education program   80%
- Have used cocaine   60%
- Involved in selling drugs   80%

The greater numbers of Hispanic and Black gang members are created by the large number of ethnicities living in lower social-economic neighborhoods where gangs are located. It is untrue that these ethnicities are predisposed to the gangster lifestyle.

7. Gang Subtypes

"Every chance we got we dissed other gangs and got away with it until the fourth or fifth time that we graffed our enemes' turf and got caught while we were rolling and bombing. They was lapped and deep and cut us off with two cars in an alley and four older vatos and one big ass black dude and they beat the shyt out of us and one of my homies had to go to the emergency room. We were lucky to get away with just a beating because we were so young. If wee had been older they might have killed one of us and we were glad to be able to get back in our hood that night."

- Taggers and tagging crews
  (Marking or painting graffiti or an individual's tag, symbol, alias, or street name)
  - Usually 12 –18 years of age.
  - Stays out all night or until early in the morning and sleeps during the day.
  - Is clandestine or deceitful about his activities.
  - Frequently carries a large backpack and wears baggy pants.
  - Has paint or felt marker stains on the tips of fingers or clothes.

- Has quantities of spray paint in cans, large felt markers, etching tools, and other graffiti, but has no reasonable explanation for having such in possession.
  - Some taggers specialize in bug spray graffiti; it only shows when wet.
- Affects a tag (street name) and writes or paints it wherever possible.
- Possesses graffiti magazines, flyers, or other portfolio of tagging.
- Displays tagging, gang marking, and other graffiti on clothing, binders, backpacks, and hats.
- Uses stylized and intertwined styles of graffiti difficult to decipher.
- Associates with children who have the traits listed above.
  - Not all taggers are gang members.
  - Some are independent operators; tagging is their insignia.
  - Some just enjoy vandalizing property.
  - Some are claiming territory much as a dog sprays mailboxes and bushes in the neighborhood.
- Often uses several tags before adopting a permanent one, and will change tag names to confuse law authorities
- Wannabe gangs
- Loosely organized group of juveniles who hang out together, manifest undesirable and anti-social behavior and acts in the community and/or school, may not even have a gang name
- Often encounter problems with real gangs for using gang names, signs, symbols, dress
- Join gangs to be cool and to intimidate

othes
- others
  - Commonly found in suburbs
  - Considered to be weekend gangsters by real gangs
  - Usually white
- Turf, or territorial gangs
  - Usually ethnic in nature
    - African-American gangs more involved in drugs and other criminal activity
    - Hispanic gangs more involved in territorial or "turf" violence
    - White and Asian gangs more involved in property crimes
  - Organize to appropriate and defend "turf"; their neighborhood
  - Occasionally embark on petty criminal activities
  - Join for protection and respect
- Criminal street gangs
  - More organized, has established a gang name
  - Seeks or has achieved gang status, reputation, and other full-blown gang attributes
  - Engages regularly in criminal activities, making money illegally
- Hardcore criminal gangs
  - Dedicated to eliminating rival gangs
  - Commit major crimes, run drugs, murder, etc.
- Prison gangs
- International gangs
- Hate gangs, racial gangs, supremacist groups
  - Have ideological or religious rational for hating members of another group

- • Engage in violence against other groups
- Motorcycle/biker gangs
- Cult groups
- Subversive groups
- Rave gangs, Party clubs/crews,

8. What Fuels Gangs?

Street gangs will defend their reputation and territory to the death, and the slightest disrespect, real or imagined, from other gang members is considered to be a slur on the honor of the entire gang and sufficient grounds for immediate and violent retaliation.

- The Three R's:
    - Respect
    - Reputation
    - Retaliation
- Gang members pride themselves on being fearless.
- To have a really bad reputation is to "have juice."
- The more "juice" they have, the more "respect" (fear) they believe they instill in others
    - Most gang violence is from gang reprisal and gang retaliation

- Retaliation drives the majority of violent gang incidents
- Intimidation of others is a major gang tactic.

The Four Gang Motives
- Honor (reputation or juice)
- Defense of turf
- Control (of what is going down)
- Gain (through criminal activity

Violence as a Gang Norm

Violence drives gang activity and is the norm in gang life. Gang violence defines the gang and the individual gang members. Many who work with gangs on the streets believe that minus violence, gangs as we know them would not exist.

Violence demonstrates bravery, manhood, and status in the gang and on the street. Gang violence allows gangs to control and expand their turf and gang activity, recruit members, settle disputes, establish the individual's role in the gang, and guarantees profits from illegal activities. Until the 1970's and 80's, criminal activity among juveniles peaked in the late teenage years. However, research shows that while juvenile crimes today reach their peak in the late teenage years, the number of violent crimes committed by youth under eighteen has increased substantially. The level of violence has increased as well. During the same time, juvenile arrest rates for drug offenses, robberies, violence, and homicides doubled. Furthermore, the number of homicides committed by juveniles with guns doubled.

This sharp increase of juvenile crime committed during this time period meshed with the introduction of rock cocaine in large American cities. Drug dealers recruited children – "shorties" -- as young as five to push their wares and encouraged, rewarded, and applauded these young criminals. Deadly weapons were suddenly available to young, confused, and impulsive young people. The combination of teenagers, guns, drugs, and gangs ushered in the sharp increase of street shootings and senseless, random murders, and increased the number of both gangs and guns into neighborhood schools.

There should be no doubt that gangs themselves accelerate criminal behavior. Studies show that gang-related children are four to six times more likely to engage in criminal behavior. As would be expected, the overwhelming amount of gang violence is perpetuated against enemy gangs; less than 15 percent is within the gangs, five percent is within the members' gangs, and a lesser amount is non-gang related

> *"when i was 15 some older dudez from school asked me to come over to one's house. When I got there they asked me some questions and wanted to know if I wanted to join their set. They told me some things about their sets and it alls ounded cool and I wanted them to like me and all Ihad to do was prove I knew hos to fight. I felt like I didn't have any choice cause they were all older and bigger than me and I wasn't doing anything anyway. Anyway, they told me to meet them the next day and four of the older dudes jumped me in but it wasn't that bad. Afterwards, I found out why they went so easy on me. There was this dude that had been causing them some problems and they wanted to send me on a mission basically to throw down on him for my mission to get into the gang. We went over to this punk's house and caught him coming home from school and I can tell you I beat the shyt out of him. Then they said I was a member and could have a gang tag and should get a tattoo showing everytbody that I was a gang member. I got one but it had to be under my shirt because my parents would have freaked out if they saw it and found out I was in a gang.*

9. Phase I - The Process of Becoming A Gang Member

Early entry into gangs
- Most gang members affiliate with gangs and become members before the age of fifteen.
- Often join gangs before they are ten or eleven; many are gang members by the time they leave elementary school. There are instances of children as young as seven claiming gang membership and involved in gang activities.
- The most reliable predictors of gang involvement are:
    - Lives in gang-infested neighborhood
    - Family member(s) in a gang
    - Family member(s) in prison
    - Confined in juvenile detention facility

Recruitment

- Each gang has its own method of recruiting almost which is a part of gang lore and in the unwritten by-laws of most gangs, and which follows a well-known cycle.
- Gangs target a likely individual for recruitment and pursue him aggressively and persistently. The individual may be a wannabe or reluctant to join the gang.
  - Individuals who stand up to the gang are the ones the gang desire most.
  - Gang invites, then harasses him to join -- or else. If he refuses, they beat him up.
  - Friends of targeted individual notice gang attention and desert the individual
  - Bereft of his support system, the individual usually yields to gang pressure
- The main recruitment pool for new gang members are the "wannabes"
  - Wannabes try to associate with gangs.
  - Assume some gang characteristics such as wearing a particular gang color.
  - Sometimes claim gang membership in an attempt to influence people in areas outside the control of the gang.
  - Wannabes are so anxious for gang recognition and membership that they often are willing to take risks that even gang members avoid, and thus can often be considered more dangerous.
  - Members 15 to 18 years old tend to be the most eager to commit risky violence -- known as "missions" in attempts to prove themselves to older gang members and raise their status within the group.

Initiation requirements

- At his initiation into the gang, the recruit must prove:
    - Love for and loyalty to the gang.
    - Commitment to lifetime affiliation with the gang.
    - Willingness to die for the gang.
        - Sometimes required conduct a "mission" of some sort, occasionally even to put his life on the line for the gang before becoming a member.
        - May be required to commit a major crime such as a drive-by shooting at rival gang members, play Russian roulette, submit to a severe physical beating, or have sex with a person with AIDS.

Initiation rituals

> *"The way I got jumped in was they told me I had to do a six penny pickup that they also called a save larry jump in. They threw six pennies on the ground and I had to get all of the pennies in one hand while they beat on me. Somebody called time on a stop watch and Tre80 and Big Macrapped starting hitting me in my face and all over and beat my ass for 60 seconds while I tried to find the pennies.   i fought back and hit Tre80 in the face and ripped out Big Mac's ear ring and busted Tre80 in the jaw they got me in my stomach and back of my head but i didn't fall down. They called time and they stopped and all gave me hugs and shook my hand and i felt loved."*

The most common forms of gang initiation are gang beatings in which the recruit is "jumped in" or, to use the Hispanic term, "cliqued in." This is often also called "going on line." This usually involves the recruit being beaten by gang members, thus giving him a chance to show his mettle by fighting back or by taking the beating without fighting back. Either way, the new recruit must continue to resist or endure the violence until the gang leadership is satisfied. Variations on this process also include:

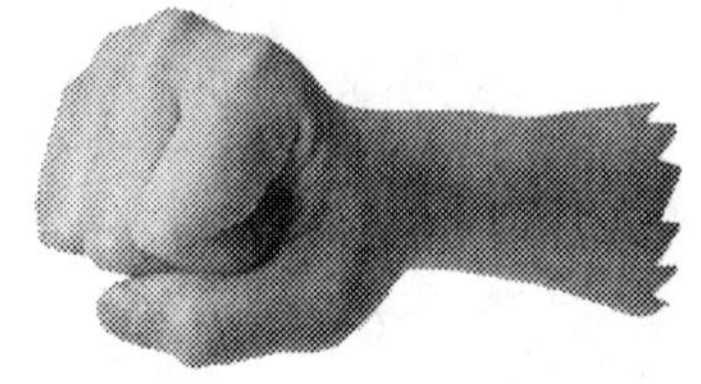

- "Walking the line" – The recruit must fight his way through a gauntlet of two lines of gang members, sometimes keeping his own hands locked behind his back while he is beaten and kicked. In some gang initiations, once the individual's knees touch the ground he is required to go back to the beginning of the gauntlet.
- Some Folk gangs use "walking the six" initiation, in which six gang members station themselves as the six points of the Star of David and beat the recruit as he walks from one to another. Blood gangs use the five-pointed star with five members stationed at each of five points.
- In Blood gangs, "jumping in" is called "blooding in."
  - There is generally no opportunity to "blood out" except by being beaten to the brink of death (and sometimes beyond) by the gang. (To use a gang expression, "Getting out of the gang is simple – if death is simple.")
  - In some large cities, the blooding-in ritual occurs in a public place, where a gang member points out an unknowing victim at random whom the recruit slashes across the face with little or no warning.

- "Quoted in" - The recruit must endure a gang beating for a quoted number of minutes.
- "Beaten in" - The recruit is not allowed to fight back, and lies in a fetal position to protect his body.
- "Circled in" - The recruit is circled by the gang and beaten until the gang is satisfied or the leaders call a halt.
- "Diseased in" - In front of the gang, the recruit must have sex with a female gang associate or prostitute with venereal disease or who is HIV positive.
- "V'd in" - same as sexed in; often refers to having sex with person with venereal disease.
- "Sexed in" - In front of the gang, the recruit must have sex with a homosexual; female affiliates are often sexed in or raped in by members of the gang in front of the gang.
- "Diced in" – A roll of the dice determines the number of minutes recruit must be beaten.
- "Flagged in" – A certain number of members put their bandanas in their back pocket and begin beating the recruit, who must fight back and capture all of the "flags".
- "Loc'ed in" - Crip initiation requiring recruit to "lock" into gang by committing crime in front of other gang members
- "Rescue Larry" – Also called Six Penny Pick Up or Rescue Hoover; six pennies are thrown on the ground and the recruit must attempt to retrieve them while being beaten. ("King" Larry Hoover, incarcerated for life in federal prison, is from Chicago, Illinois, the land of Lincoln; Lincoln's head is on a penny;

also, the "bars" on the back of a penny represent the jail holding Hoover.)
- Twenty-Six Penny Pick Up – Same as Six Penny Pick Up, initiation into Two-Sixers gang; considered more violent initiation for tougher, older gang members.
- "Blessed in" - On rare occasions, a person who has rendered unusual and valuable service to the gang - provided guns, committed perjury to get a gang member off a murder charge - will be "blessed" into the gang without a beating. Often the service to the gang involves doing a drive-by shooting, after which the "blessing in" occurs only after the recruit, on hands and knees, answers several questions about the gang culture.
- "Courted in" – Same as blessed in, except gang extends membership to person they want to do favors for the gang.
- "Walled in" - recruit faces a wall while he is beaten by gang members.
- "Drive by-ed" - recruit has to shoot someone, preferably a member of an enemy gang, usually in a drive-by shooting.

10. Phase II - Immersion Into the Gang

Gang Identity

- Once accepted into the gang, the new member usually adopts a nickname (moniker) or street name and uses it exclusively on the streets and in graffiti and tattoos.
- This practice is so prevalent that often members of the same gang will not even know each other's legal names.
- The nicknames can often:
  - Give insight into a member's psychological perspective of himself (e.g., Crazy, Killer).
  - Indicate physical description (e.g., Tank, Treetop, Flaco, Gordo.
- Often the first letter of the real name connected to a gang term is used, such as C-Bone or B-Loc.
- Many require the new member to tattoo the gang's names and/or gang symbols, logos, or initials on their bodies.

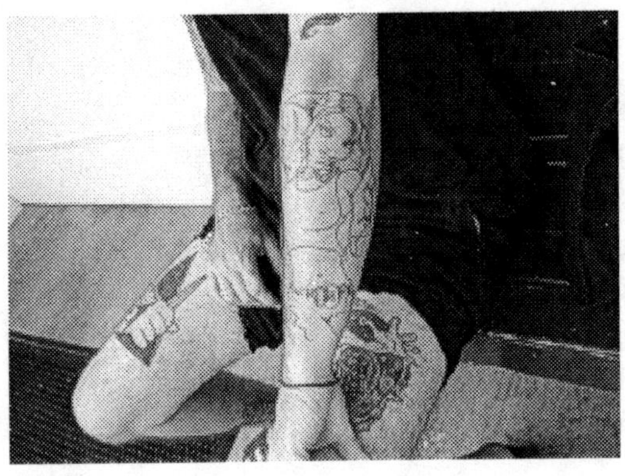

Gang Colors and Other Gang Identifiers

Traditionally, certain colors have served as gang identifiers. However, they also hinder gang activities by drawing attention and announcing gang presence and affiliation. During recent years, some older gang members have begun to disguise their gang ties by wearing different colors to blend in the general population, so they cannot be easily connected to their gangs. Still, the younger the gang member and the newer his status with the gang, the more likely he will be to flaunt and use traditional gang colors, styles, numbers, slogans, and other identifiers.

> *"I wore my best clothes to my new school, and soon knew I had made a mistake cause I was geared down in my gang's light blue and everybody in the halls looks at me weird and one guy asks if I am new, and tells me red and black are the only colors to wear to this school. I knew I had made a mistake and had to adjust, so I told them I was new and the next day I changed colors and now I am banging for red and black. From that day on I sported only those colors because if I didn't I would have been beaten up each day."*

- In the wrong place, the wrong neighborhood, or the wrong situation, wearing gang colors and attire can put an unsuspecting young person in serious danger and could even result in his death at the hands of a real gang angered by his "false flagging" or by enemy gangs of that particular color.
- Parents who do not want their children mistaken for gang members by the clothes they wear should keep gangs' affiliation with certain colors in mind when shopping for their children's clothes.

- Parents should be concerned when their child does not want to give up a certain article of clothes, especially if it is one of the few colors-- or the only color--he likes to wear.
- The new gang member must display prominently at all times the primary personal accessories that identify gang affiliation, such as certain colors, hats, handkerchiefs, shoe laces, belts, buckles, and haircuts.
- When a gang is on the prowl for enemy gang members and the hunt proves unsuccessful, they will often harm anyone wearing the enemy's colors, resulting in danger from gang assaults on innocent persons.

Gang Lore

- After being jumped in, the new member is indoctrinated with an "All for One, One for All" mentality that demands complete devotion to that gang set and nation.
- Most codes of conduct require lifetime allegiance to the group.
- He also must memorize alliance and set history, organization, and mythical symbolism referred to as "knowledge."
- This "knowledge" is often copied and passed around by members/prospective members.
- The writings are often coded or cryptic and make use of a specific alphabet.
- The recruit is required to know by rote the gang's history and to relate it when called upon by an older member of the gang. This is called to "spit the lit."

Gang Discipline

- The new member also must learn and follow a strict set of gang rules.
  - Above all, he must follow all orders given by gang leaders. (One interpretation of the acronym FOLKS is "Follow All Laws the King Speaks".)
  - Breaking one of these laws triggers a "violation" and punishment decided by gang leaders
    - Minor violations, such as being late for a meeting or speaking out of turn or interrupting when another person is speaking during a business meeting, can result in the offender being "violated" by having to pay a fine, perform menial tasks for the gang, or receive a brief beating from a designated gang member.
    - Major violations, such as those reflecting poorly on the individual or the gang or compromising the gang's honor or activities, usually merit severe physical assault for a set period of time or in a prescribed manner, such as a certain number of blows to the chest, generally no more than five to ten at a time. "Fifty to the Chest" is usually a death sentence.

Gang Rivalries

- The new gang member automatically assumes the friendships and rivalries of the gang and the sets with which the gang is aligned.
- Often this means aligning with nationally-known "nations" such as the Folk Nation or the People Nation

- Nation-aligned sets are deadly rivals, and as such are enemies of all who belong to enemy gangs.
- Loyalties can be as simple a matter as one gang (Crips) automatically accepting as an ally any gang that considers Bloods an enemy, and vice versa.

Gang Communication

- Gang communications may take different forms, and usually involve particular behavior, hand or other signals, colors, clothing, guns, jewelry, symbols, graffiti, specialized alphabet, gang and street slang, and tattoos.
- The new member becomes proficient in communicating by "throwing up the signs" and "stacking the signs."
- He also learns to use vocabulary, terms, signs, and symbols peculiar to his gang.
- Since gang identifiers are forbidden in the penal system, incarcerated gang members when asked to represent will simply say "Folks" or "People."

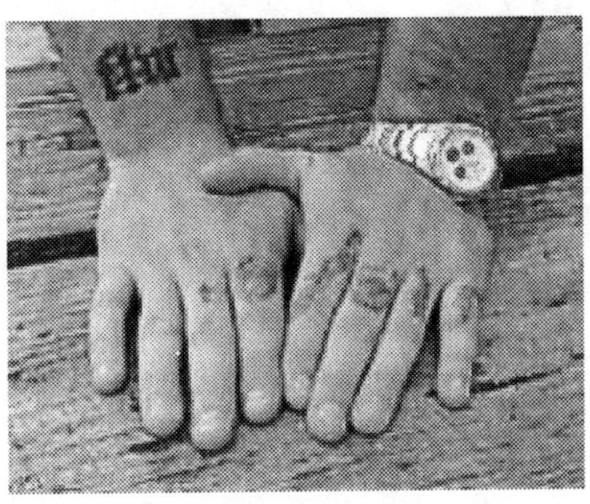

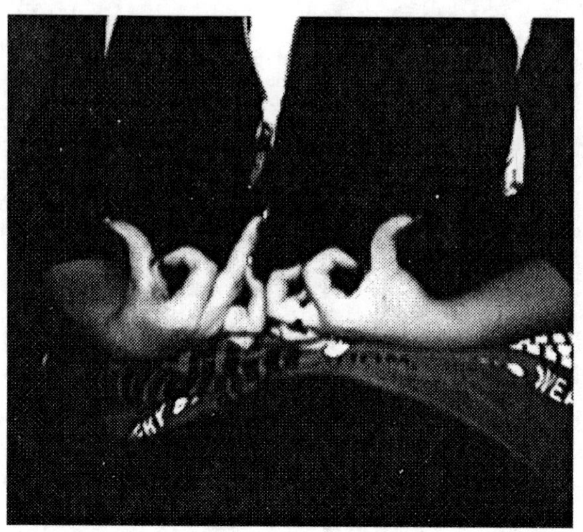

- This has spread to the streets, where gang members, when told to represent, will say, "I'm repping People", or "I'm repping Folks", to identify their particular gangs. "Repping" means to represent, favor, or use one side of the body to the exclusion of the other side of the body.
- Gang members have their own particular rules for speaking or writing to a "homeboy", which is another name for a fellow gang member.
- Gang members may refer to their organization as a:
  - nation
  - family
  - hood
  - set
  - posse
  - crew
  - clique
  - dawg pound (Blood gangs)
  - flu crew (Crip gangs)

Gang Status

- The new member strives to elevate his status through several stages of gang membership. Some gang experts classify these stages as:
    - The "fantasy" level of being intrigued and fascinated with gangs, followed by
    - The "wannabe" stage, which speaks for itself
    - Next is the "affiliate" stage, during which he associates with the gang and does gang business, but is not yet a member
    - As a new member, he is often called a BG (baby gangster); younger juvenile members are called TGs (tiny gangsters)
    - Then to full-fledged "gangster", a hard-core member who acts and talks independently within the gang milieu, and commits criminal acts
    - Finally becoming an "Old Time Gangster" or OG -- "Original Gangster"
    - Gang members hold OGs in especially high regard, since they are likely to be the originators of the set who have earned their reputations
    - The younger gang members are controlled by the OGs and refer respectfully to them as "shot callers"
    - As gang members become older, some will assume a more sedentary lifestyle while maintaining their gang affiliation. Thus distanced from daily association with younger and more active gang members, the gang activities of these "veteranos" tend to decrease

Several unique terms are used interchangeably for leaving the gang to join another gang or leaving gangism permanently. "Getting divorced", "dropping the flag", or "flipping" are generally not options -- once in, always in, unless expelled, usually with a beating or in death. This expectation of lifetime commitment to the gang is expressed in such common statements as, "Kill to join, die to quit", and "If it is easy to die, then it is easy to get out of a gang", and "There is only one way out of the gang, and that's in a body bag."

While a veterano may "go underground" or "chill" to distance himself from active gang activities and over time become a respected alumni and/or adult advisor, an active gang member who wishes to desert one gang for another or leave the gang life altogether often must relocate to another community where his former gang does not exist and his former gang membership is not known.

Peripherals who associate with gangs

- "Associates" will often identify with gang members in their neighborhood, but some seldom involve themselves deeply with gang activity.
  - Dope suppliers and fences would be examples of associates
  - Others outside the gang who identify with the gang for protection or for favors. This group mainly consists of women, who are used to carry drugs or guns for members in return for money or drugs. (All-female gangs do exist and are on the increase, but they have little status with male gangs.)

11. Gang Presence and Activities

- Baggy jeans and the gangbanger look have been adopted by some young people as fashion statements, and do not necessarily mean gangs have arrived at your school. However, the origin of "sagging and bagging" was to conceal weapons and drugs, and the style still serves that purpose for gang members
- Graffiti on buildings, curbs, car washes, street signs, parks, public and school bathrooms
- Presence of groups of youths affecting gang behavior, dress, and activity
- Growing citizen complaints of youth groups causing fear and intimidation in the area
- Rumors of gang activity and fights
- Fighting between groups of young people
- Escalation of crimes, especially crimes of violence
- Senseless violence
- Growing vandalism, auto thefts, robberies, muggings, break-ins, and burglaries

- Crimes committed with weapons
- Increase in drug trafficking and use

Predictable pattern of gang violence

Gang violence follows a regular and predictable pattern. In some cases, gangs feel they must avenge an assault or violation of their honor within a set time period, such as twenty-four hours, and announce that the "clock is locked". This means that the gang will retaliate within the established time period, usually twenty-four hours, and will make every effort to find and injure an enemy gang member.

- Gang experiences real or perceived threat from rival gang
- Gang mobilizes, organizes for action against rival gang
- Escalation of gang activity, intruding into other gang's territory, increase in graffiti
- Incident (usually dissing)
- Retaliation (usually violent)
- Retaliating gang goes into hiding
- Other gang seeks revenge, violent incidents occur

- Retaliation goes into continuous loop between the two gangs

The hours that the clock is locked are particularly dangerous for not only the enemy gang but also innocent citizens who might be wearing the enemy gang's colors. As the time passes and the deadline draws near, the gang's anxiety over saving honor by injuring an enemy gang member builds, and often culminates with assault on anyone wearing the enemy color. Although the person injured or killed is not an enemy gang member, the gang can claim their honor intact because they have assaulted the enemy color … and who knows whether the person was an enemy gang member or not.

Indicators of Impending Gang Violence

This requires school personnel who have a skill for gang awareness and almost a sixth sense.
If the violence occurs in a school, almost invariably some students know it is going to happen.

- Increase in graffiti, dissing of graffiti, symbols, signing.

- Increase in flaunting of gang items, caps, rags, colors; gang members "dripping" in colors.
- Gang groups roam the campus, often affecting a strutting behavior and intimidating and bullying non-gang students.
- Rival gangs "appropriate turf"; establish areas that others begin to avoid.
- Gang's behavior becomes purposeful; members begin looking around warily, over shoulders.
- Intended area of confrontation suddenly becomes vacated; students not involved go elsewhere or move to the sides to watch.
- Often girls who are gang associates are seen loitering nearby, watching with intense interest; they may appear to be waiting for something to happen, and are usually carrying items such as coats, book bags
- "Maddogging" and stare-downs intensify; more challenging stances, swaggering walks, aggressive speech, signs thrown
- Escalation of gang signs, gang slogans, shrill gang whistles
- Symbolic challenge issued; gang members stand out in front of their gang, shrug their shoulders and arms up, signals such as pulling at the shoulders of the shirt
- Verbal challenges issued: "What's up?"; "Do you want to ride?"
- Gang walks purposefully and in concert, and then run to attack the other gang

12. Solving The Problem

Ten Stratigies For Parents And Teachers

1. Remember that children want, need, and expect
    clear limits on their activities.
    - Establish clear, fair, and reasonable boundaries,
      rules, and expectations.
    - Set consequences for violations.
    - Do the right thing for your child, even if it hurts.
    - Do not yield to protests such as "But, Mom,
      everybody gets to do that!" (Answer: "Then *you*
      will be the exception.")
    - Make the call; *you* are the parent.
    - Stick to your decisions.
    - Do not try to be the "nice guy"; it makes a
      mockery of your disciplinary efforts in your
      child's eyes.

2. Do not allow children to attend or host
    unsupervised activities, especially parties
    - Give your child a touchstone rule by which to
      live, such as:
      Be *where* you are supposed to be,
      When you are supposed to be,
      With whom you are supposed to be,
      Doing *what* you are supposed to be doing.

3. Develop open lines of communication with your
    child.
    - Talk and listen frequently, openly, and positively.
    - Use humor whenever possible
    - Spend time with your child; keep him busy and
      occupied.
    - Assign home responsibilities.
    - Involve him in after-school activities.

- Eliminate "just hanging out" time with friends.
- If your child attends an activity, know when, where, what, and with whom he will be at all times.
- Be certain that reliable adult supervision is present at activities.
- Take him to church, children's, and youth activities.
- Help him find, work at, and learn from an after-school job.
- Participate in your child's education; attend his events.
- Emphasize that school and grades are important.

4. Considering your child's level of maturity, responsibility, and truthfulness, establish a reasonable curfew for weekend and holiday evening activities, such as:
   - No later than 9:00 - 10:00 for children under 16
   - No later than 10:00 - 11:00 for children under 17
   - No later than 11:00 - 12:00 for children under 18.

5. Know your child's friends.
   - Meet his friends, especially if he does not want you to meet them.
   - Find out what they look like, talk about, how they spend their free time.
   - Try to ascertain what influence they have over him.
   - Meet and interact with their parents.

6. Discourage your child from any involvement with gangs by:
   - Discussing the negatives of gang affiliation
   - Stressing that gangs are dangerous

- Convincing him that he is an important part of the family
- Teaching him your values.

7. Ask questions about gang activity.
   - Do you know what gangs are and what they do?
   - Are there any gangs at your school or in the community?
   - Do you know any gang members?
   - Has a gang ever approached you in any way?
   - Are you in a gang?

8. Teach your child what to do if gang members approach
   - Do not respond to gang contacts.
   - Do not make eye contact.
   - Do not be around gang members or in gang areas at any time.
   - Best response is just to walk away.

9. Warn your child he must not:
   - Attempt, even in jest or play, "false flagging" (display by non-gang member of any kind of gang signing, language or symbol)
   - Wear gang-related clothing
   - Draw, write, or practice gang writing or gang names, messages, or graffiti; especially on or in:
     - Books/Notebooks
     - Paper
     - Clothes
     - Book bags
     - His own body
     - Other belongings
     - Rooms
     - *Anywhere!*

10. Watch for changes indicating gang involvement.
- <u>Behavior</u>
    - Has diminishing grades, poor attendance, and behavior problems.
    - Drops out of family, school, sports, church, and other activities.
    - Shows interest in gangster-influenced music, behavior, writing, talking.
    - Imitates or affects gang attitude, writing, symbols, signs, behavior, clothes.
    - Shows signs of use of alcohol and other drugs
    - Has an abrupt change in personality, behavior, and overall attitude.
    - Demonstrates violent behavior or threatens violent behavior.
    - Develops an interest in guns and other weapons.
    - Carries a weapon, or is obsessed with weapons.
    - Begins to develop streetwise vocabulary, behavior.
    - Evidences hatred of other groups or persons for no apparent reason.
    - Develops unusual desire for privacy and secrecy.
    - Rearranges room or living quarters to create more privacy.
    - Is arrested, or friends or associates are arrested.
    - Does everything to the left or right ("orientation").
    - Says he is "hanging around", but does not explain.
    - Possesses gang literature.

- Possesses photographs showing gang games, gang slogans, gang insignias, or gang activities.
- Becomes defiant toward authority, often violent toward parents, teachers, others.
- Brags about or struts about his new gang status.
- Eager to gain reputation of being "bad"; fights willingly, unnecessarily.
- Often is not where supposed to be.
- Sneaks out of house.
- Often spends evenings away from home without permission.
- <u>Symbols</u>
  - Wears personal property with gang symbols.
  - Gang tattoos
  - Has new haircut with stripes or patterns cut into hair
  - Writes or draws gang graffiti on notebooks or belongings.
  - Has gang photographs, books, posters, and graffiti in bedroom, especially on bedroom walls.
- <u>Dress</u>
  - Seems obsessed with just one or two particular colors of clothing; will wear no other colors.
  - Wears gang clothing, styles, and colors.
  - Wears belt buckle or other accessory with initial not his own.
  - Favors one particular professional team logo or uniform.
  - Wears sagging pants.
  - Affects gang dress.
  - Wears all clothes, jewelry, and other

accessories "repping" to the left or the right.
- Wears head covering, hood, bandana, etc., with gang colors or repping to one side
- Has gang symbols inside cap or on underside of brim.
- Wears belt buckle, sometimes military style buckle, with initial not his own.
- <u>Money, Jewelry</u>
  - Wears excessive jewelry with distinctive designs or with gang symbols.
  - Wears beads in same color as clothes.
  - Affects right or left orientation in jewelry, colors, and other items. (Does everything to right or left.)
  - Suddenly possesses unexplained cash, clothing, jewelry, and other items.
  - Showers wealth on friends, family.
  - Frequently requests to borrow money.
- <u>Physical Changes</u>
  - Has unexplained physical injuries (such as being beaten), or lies about events surrounding the injuries.
  - Has injuries to body, but not to face. (Injuries inflicted during gang initiations are often deliberately on the recruit's body so they will be less obvious than injuries to the face and other exposed areas.)
  - Appears proud of injuries.
  - Has peculiar drawings or language on personal belongings or on body.
  - Has a tattoo or "brand."
  - Affects a particular hairstyle common to a few.
  - Has gang signs cut into hair.
  - Head shaved, bald, or hair extremely short.

- Has slashes cut into eyebrows.
  - Shows changes in physical appearance.
  - Often drowsy, eyes red, swollen, speech blurred.
- <u>Family</u>
  - Withdraws from family.
  - Becomes increasingly defiant.
  - Breaks family rules.
  - Refers to new friends as "family".
- <u>Friends</u>
  - Undesirable friends and associates replace previous desirable friends and associates
  - New friends either do not visit or are secretive when they do
  - Are usually males with unusual, unexplained first names
  - New friends all wear same colors or sports clothing or indicate gang affiliation in other ways.
  - Attend functions sponsored or attended by known gang members.
  - Loiter, ride, meet, or hang out with gang members.
  - Have undesirable influences with/from unknown sources, have negative role models
  - Are streetwise, anti-social, hostile, aggressive
  - Lack respect for parents; break parental and school rules consistently.
  - Have loose family ties, inadequate family attention and supervision
  - Are victims of abuse or neglect
  - Often are from economically/socially deprived backgrounds
  - Have low or diminishing grades, poor attendance, or are dropouts

Handling Gang Members in School

- Establish a zero tolerance policy for any violence -- and especially for parent and student abuse of school staff
- Educate your faculty and staff about gangs.
- Gang members do not come to school to get a formal education, but to:
    - Use the school as a stage on which they can strut their gang culture
    - Impress and intimidate their peers and school personnel
    - Flaunt their gang membership, colors, signs, other gang identification
    - Congregate and discuss their activities in a social arena
    - Uphold their reputation as an established gang
    - Display their strength of membership
    - Recruit potential members
    - Challenge other gangs in an atmosphere of adult supervision
    - Commit criminal or violent acts with little concern for law enforcement and even less for school personnel
    - Avoid arrest for violation of school attendance laws
- Gangs have their own recognizable culture and ways of communicating
- Enlist help of your faculty and staff to develop a plan to handle gang activity.
    - Discourage giving undue media attention to gangs; it can actually encourage gang membership.

- Remember that gang members, like all adolescents, need to feel special in some way, and hunger for recognition.
- Remember that gang members lack the tools to deal appropriately with conflict.
- Do not sanction or broker truces or negotiations with, between, or among gangs! To do so gives gangs, recognition, credibility and power.
- Do not use gang members to assist school with gang problems.
- Enforce the law and place gang members in alternative schools; if necessary, ban gang members from school activities and school property except for alternative programs.
- Provide counseling and mentors for gang members.
- Locate and utilize dependable people in the community who have rapport with gangs and intimate knowledge about them.
- Use faculty members who are able to deal successfully with gangs. (Research has shown that almost every gang member remembers with fondness at least one teacher they had in grades K-6, while few remember any teacher with fondness after sixth grade.)
- Let teachers work with the educational problems, and call in law enforcement officers to work with the criminal problems.
- Maintain an adequate and visible presence of law officers (gang members have more respect for officers of the law but will challenge security officers) at school and at all school events.

- Establish an environment that is not conducive to gang activity
- Develop clear and consistent rules that are firm, fair, and few.
- Post, explain, and disseminate the rules and expectations to students and parents
- Establish and maintain order, discipline, and control on the first day of school
- Deal with infractions and disruptions appropriately, quickly, firmly, fairly
- Create and maintain well-managed and well-organized halls and classrooms
- Work effectively with parents so that their children meet academic and behavioral expectations
- Use a variety of teaching methods effectively to keep interest and engagement high
- Recognize and provide for students' cultural diversity and learning styles
- Know how to defuse disruptive, violent, frustrated, angry behavior
- Require and strive for academic success for all
- Understand that most gang activities are carried out in the neighborhood and not in the school; most gang problems that occur at school originate in the streets
- Be realistic; sometimes you have to determine whether to focus on preventing gang activity at the school or on simply reducing gang activity

- Develop a positive school philosophy about gangs such as:

The school campus is a neutral and safe place for all. The only gang allowed here is Our High School Gang. All students belong to our gang. Anyone who engages in unacceptable behavior will be subject to immediate disciplinary action.

- Teach faculty and staff how to deal effectively with gang members
    - Respond to aggressive acts by gang members only with support staff --never alone.
    - Remember that you are the adult … insist on respect, but give what respect and courtesy you can while interacting.
    - Do not unnecessarily intrude into a gang member's personal space.
    - Never allow gang members to intimidate you.
    - Do not attempt to intimidate gang members; it will lead to confrontation
    - Be decisive, firm, and fair.
    - Remember that gangs view leniency as weakness
    - Never let gang members know your level of gang knowledge
    - Know how to identify early gang behavior.
    - Do not become defensive; do not deny or ignore that the student is a gang member.

- Interact voluntarily on an informal basis; duty teachers in informal settings are usually somewhat successful.
- Understand cultural mores that may complicate the situation, such as the objection of some Hispanic males to take orders from a female
- Initial contacts should be brief, positive, and conducted in front of the gang.
- Never call a gang member by his street name; know and use his real name.
- Never use gang language; it legitimizes the lifestyle.
- Never give a gang member an ultimatum in front of anyone else.
- Never lie to a gang member.
- Never touch a gang member in public or private unless absolutely necessary.
- Never unnecessarily challenge a gang member in public or private
- Never put a gang member in a situation in which he has to "act out" in front of others to save face.
- Examine notebooks, papers, folders, and textbooks for gang graffiti.
- Confiscate and turn in to administrators any gang graffiti or items.
- Never allow graffiti, gang or otherwise, on school papers
- Talking with gang members:
  - Conduct formal business with a gang member in private and in a formal setting. Do not take notes while talking with a gang member; make mental notes instead.

- At first discuss school progress, social activities, family, etc.
- If possible, establish a connection. ("I taught your sister/know your father/live down the street from you/see you at work.")
- If a gang member is inclined to talk, appear interested; gang members like to brag.
- Try to be as understanding as possible; may cause gang member to be more open and cooperative.
- Make a sympathetic connection such as, "I know most people don't understand the gang thing. You're not a bad guy. How can I help you out? I don't want to see you get into trouble. How can we work this out?"
- Use the gang's dislike for enemy gangs. They will tell you nothing about their own gang, but will often speak freely about the enemy.
- Discuss gang membership only after you have established a relationship.
- Present alternatives to gang membership as positives, without mentioning gang relationships.

- With assistance of coaching staff, channel aggressive gang members into athletics.
- Avoid media attention, which may actually escalate gang activity; gangs love this type of attention. If possible, ask media to not report name of gangs involved in incidents; such publicity spurs rival gangs to strive for equal attention.

- If it becomes necessary to have gang
  members arrested, have it done in private;
  gang members glory in public arrest and jail,
  trials, and prison terms provide them with
  widespread publicity and instant prestige in
  the eyes of the gang community.
- Inform parents of the student's gang
  affiliation, in the hope of dissuading gang
  membership. (Educators have an obligation
  to inform parents. This works better at lower
  levels than at middle and high school.)
- Keep a file folder on all suspected/known
  gang actions; document persons, times,
  places, incidents. Patterns will emerge that
  can be helpful in tracking and preventing
  gang activity on campus.
- Separate members of same gangs in
  classrooms
- Keep rival gangs apart in class whenever
  possible.
- Keep members of same gangs out of same
  classes whenever possible.
- Share all gang incidents and behaviors with
  parents.

Practical Tips for Practical Principals

Parents may forgive educators if they do not educate their children well, but they will never forgive them if they do not return their children safely at the end of each school day.

(On Campus)

- If an area isn't being used, lock it!
- Hire adequate numbers of counselors and crisis counselors.
- Create a school environment that is inviting and in which every student knows he/she is important and valued.
- Institute a character education course that is embedded in the curriculum and summarized in the advisory, teaches conflict resolution techniques, and emphasizes values, morals, and ethics.
- Offer education about gangs to students, preferably in small groups conducive to discussion, emphasizing that gangs are destructive and dangerous. Present techniques that will help students to avoid becoming involved with gangs. Make students aware of opportunities for and rewards of involvement in positive group experiences.
- Identify students who are vulnerable to gang involvement, and provide them with special mentoring, conflict resolution training, peer counselors, support groups, tutors, and opportunities for involvement in the school activity program.
- Provide programs that will assist all school staff, parents, and outside agencies to understand how gangs develop and how to respond to them.

- These programs should take into consideration the diversity of the community, and be presented in a manner sensitive to the various cultures that may be present, if needed in the languages of the parents and community.
- Adopt, post, disseminate, and enforce a policy that provides a campus free of drugs, violence, weapons, and gangs.
- Use an effective Student Assistance Program.
- Provide Stay Safe training for all personnel and students.
- Establish an "eye contact network" so duty personnel are always within eye contact of one another.
- Employ electronic communication equipment such as classroom emergency telephones or call buttons, radios, cell telephones, and alpha pagers.
- Establish after-care programs that help keep younger students off the street and with after-school supervision and programs.
- Investigate the positive aspects of standard dress for students.
- Prepare the staff to recognize and prevent violence. Hire role models, and provide teachers of same race/ethnicity as students.
- Hire teachers who will live in the community, to help reweave the torn fabric of the community.
- Teach basic skills of courtesy and respect for others to all ages and at all levels; teach children how to react appropriately toward others.
- Engage school, family, and community in solving the problem.
- Institute advisory periods for all grades.
- Use parent patrols, Mom and Dad Helpers on campus.

- Look for signs of gang involvement and activity, especially on Mondays and after holidays.
- Institute conflict resolution and anger management programs.
- Involve every student in meaningful, successful extracurricular programs.
- Develop an honor code for behavior in school.
- Initiate student or teen court.
- Create safe corridors, safe campus programs.
- Establish a School Crime Stoppers program.

(Off Campus)

Enlist assistance and cooperation of local agencies
- Promote the image of law enforcement officer as a friend, helper, and protector.
- Place law enforcement resource officers on campus.
- Know what a school resource officer is supposed to do and do not diminish his role or authority; he is a law enforcement officer, not a security person. (There is quite a difference!)
- Keep in mind that educators are trained to deal with discipline problems whereas school resource officers and other law enforcement personnel are trained to deal with criminal behavior.
- Bring trained safety officers into the schools for drug, traffic, and citizenship education.
- Request increased police patrols in the school area.
- Request a school safety audit and a gang presence audit by a trained law enforcement gang specialist.
- Ask police to monitor youths who are not enrolled in school but who "hang out" on or near

school property. This can help school officials assess the existence of gangs in the neighborhood, and anticipate and prevent their formation in the school.
* Add security personnel for parking lots, hallways, and other common areas.
* Invite law enforcement groups to train in your school (SWAT teams, building searches).
* Have a MOU (memo of understanding) between the school district and police so everyone will know what should happen when police arrive.
* Practice clear responses to intruders to the campus, and to intoxicated, abusive, aggressive, hostile, or just plain rude people.
* Maintain information on gang activity and share it with police officers.
* Provide free admittance to school activities for law officers and their immediate families to build relationships and good will.

What Concerned Communities Can Do to Prevent Gangs

* Build partnerships with law enforcement, other agencies for interventions, (religious, recreational, social services, public housing, health agencies, business community, and law enforcement.)
* Educate the parents and community.
* Provide accurate information.
* Build common agreement and common goals.
* Sponsor programs about:
  * Parenting
  * Improving family relationships
  * Conflict resolution
  * Anger management

- Self- and job improvement programs (GED, skills programs).
- Coordinate community athletic and social events, holiday celebrations, proms, graduations, and other important functions.
- Promote community and parent associations, athletic leagues, and community fairs.
- Obtain business partnerships for teams, bands, chess clubs, fine arts, and other programs after school.
- Create safe routes and havens to and from school.
- Institute a Safe Home Agreement for parents.
- Encourage news media to cover positive stories about accomplishments of young people.
- Help in breaking family cycles of violence and poverty.

Importance of Gang Identification

Since gangs adopt particular colors, types and styles of dress, and numerous other ways of setting themselves apart from others while promoting solidarity among the gang, it is important to be able to correctly identify gang members using these means.

Those in charge of young people (schools, law enforcement, etc.) should be familiar with gang identification procedures and should never ignore such displays of gang membership. Once something has been definitely identified as being gang-related, it should be discouraged with explanations of the problem and specifically denied to gang members by written notification. Whenever possible, a report of such gang activity should be made to the local law enforcement agencies, a written record made of the incident and the warning or ban, including a picture whenever possible.

Ignoring gang behaviors, clothes, or paraphernalia sends a powerful message that those in charge or either not knowledgeable about gangs, are unable or unwilling to prevent a gang presence in the area. This inevitably results in the gangs feeling free to conduct gang business, recruit from other young people in the area, and to become more powerful and difficult to control in the future.

13. Writing On The Wall: Gang Graffiti

Appropriate Reaction to Graffiti

- Read it
- Record it
- Report it
- Remove it
- Research it
- Remember it

Anti-Graffiti Laws

Graffiti has been classified in some communities as a separate crime. In Texas, criminal penalties have been increased for those who graffiti.

Texas Penal Code Section 28:08 (September 1, 1999) states that:

A person commits an offense if with aerosol paint or an indelible marker, an etching, or engraving device and without the effective consent of the owner the person intentionally or knowing makes markings,

Purpose and use of graffiti

Graffiti is defined as a …
crude drawing or inscription scratched on a wall or other surface, usually as to be seen by the public.
(American Heritage Dictionary)

It is one way of keeping up with which gangs are in the area, their locations within the community, the names of their members, the identity of their enemies, and their activities, including drug sales and violence or intended violence.

Someone familiar with graffiti can often tell whether it is gang related, the work of taggers, or merely teenage anti-social behavior by individuals seeking notoriety and attention.

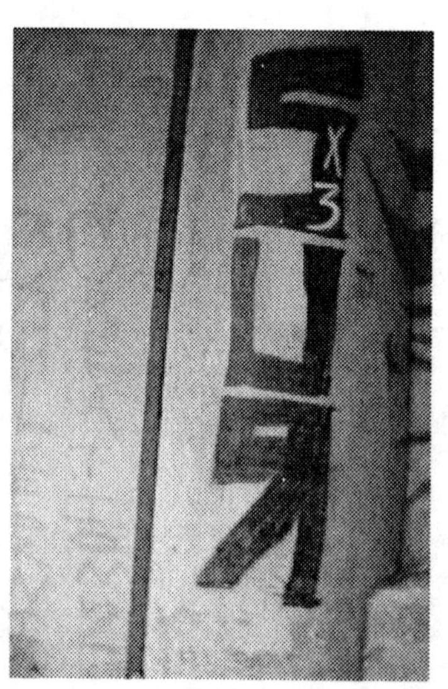

The appearance of gang graffiti in the community is proof there is at least one gang member in the area. However, if other rival gangs are already present, one or a few new gang members tend to delay "graffing" to avoid getting caught or outnumbered at these primary locations. This is especially true if the area or the new gang is secluded.

Example of gang graffiti indicating the letter "M"
for an Hispanic group
(XIII the 13th letter of the alphabet), area code
(254), Surenos (a California gang), and
"Gangsta" title (G).

Unchecked, gangs will usually mark up their entire neighborhood with graffiti, including fences, schools, sidewalks, walls, vehicles, and even homes to claim the area as their turf. Primary hangouts of the gangs, especially the walls, signs, sidewalks, and streets, usually will be heavily covered with graffiti.

Gang graffiti is used by gangs as an informal bulletin board or newsletter to:
- Communicate and send messages
  - To other gangs
  - Not to the general public
- Declare the gang's existence and presence in the community
- Identify the gang
  - Name of the gang
  - Size of the gang
  - Ethnic makeup of the gang
  - Membership and their names

- Communicate territorial limits and mark turf to define area claimed by the gang
- Claim affiliation with other gangs
- Advertise and glorify the gang and its exploits
  - Drug sales
  - Possession/use/type of weapons
  - Violence
- Issue challenges and announce warnings of future acts and retaliation
- Show disrespect to enemy gangs
  - This can be considered a killing offense by the gangs
  - Simply crossing out other gang's graffiti may lead to serious retaliation
- Eulogize and memorialize slain gang members

Gangs have favorite places, areas, or items to "tag" with graffiti.
- Mail and neighborhood postage boxes
- Parking meters
- Billboards
- Street and highway signs
- Freeway overpasses and concrete ramps and abutments
- Rest rooms
- Public walls
- Fences
- Neighborhood marquees and signs
- Dumpsters
- Garbage cans
- Public park tables and benches
- Railroad cars
- Train stations
- Tractor trailers

Major types of graffiti

- Tagging
    a. Marking or painting gang graffiti or an individual's tag, symbol, alias, or street name
    b. Can be considered an autograph of the tagger or gang member
    c. Intended to announce presence and attract attention
    d. Requires minimum of expertise, equipment, time, or effort
    e. Has little artistic intent or merit
    f. Experienced taggers can accomplish extensive tagging in just a few seconds, and can do so repeatedly in public with little chance of being caught.
- Bombing
    a. Accomplished within a few minutes
    b. Has been compared to handing out business cards or flyers
    c. Usually only one or two color scheme
    d. May have some artistic merit
    e. Large murals painted or marked with the utmost of care

f.   Could be likened to artistic advertising
g.   Intended to show pride in the graffiti
h.   Involves many hours, copious amounts of several colors of paint or markers

- Piecing
    a.   A masterpiece – "a piece" – is graffiti that takes considerable time and talent. It usually is on a large surface such as a wall, the side of a building, or an overpass. Large overhead areas seen for quite a distance are favorite spots for "pieces".

- Ethnic Graffiti
- Black gang graffiti
    - Usually written left to right and top to bottom
    - Often crudely drawn with rounded outline of letters
    - Less sophisticated, less detail
    - Often includes the $ (dollar sign) as indication of drugs for sale
    - Often uses the slant sign (/) for the space between words or letters, as V/L or Vice Lords
    - Often substitutes words for numbers, as "one eight trey" for 183
    - Will generally glorify the individual first and the gang second
    - Street names intended to inspire fear, such as "Killer" or "Monster".
    - Generally the individual's name or moniker will be in large capital letters; the gang name and those of associates will be written in very small letters
    - Numbers will be substituted for letters of the alphabet

- 2 - 4 - Black Gangsters
- 2-4-7-14 - BGDN (Black Gangster Disciple Nation)

- White gang graffiti
  - Often contains names of punk and heavy metal groups
  - May include lines from songs published by those types of groups, satanic and devil worship symbols
  - May make reference to drug sales or use
  - White graffiti is generally not used to mark territory
  - Instead, it announces the white gang's presence in the community
  - Will often use gang names that end with "Boys", "Posse", "Gangsters", or "Crew"

- Hispanic gang graffiti
  - Called *placas* (postings)
  - Usually includes words in Spanish, such as:
    - puto - male prostitute
    - rata -snitch, informant
    - locos - crazy people
  - Gang member's street names often relate to physical characteristics, such as "Flaco" (thin) or "Chino" (slant eyes)
  - English words often spelled incorrectly according to how they sound in Spanish, such as Ge-ache or G.H. for Green Hills; Ve-e-ele-ese - Vel's for Varrio Encanto Locos
  - Often includes symbols, letters, or numbers of the letters in the alphabet to abbreviate gang affiliation, such as "M" or "EME" for 13; "N" for "ENE" or 14.

Decoding Graffiti

- Do not attempt to read all of the graffiti at once
- Identify the style used in form the letters in the graffiti
    - Circled
    - Square
    - Diamond
    - Half diamond
    - Crooked
    - Waved
    - Looped
    - Backwards
    - Upside down
- Break it down into small parts

Steps for Graffiti Analysis:

1. Try to identify the gang by clues in the graffiti
    - Actual gang names (Vice Lords, Bloods, etc.)
    - Initials of the gang (VL, B, BD)
    - Gang symbols (five-pointed star, glove, champagne glass, etc.)
    - Gang numbers (3, 5, 6 7, 2.7.4, 12-12-12, etc.)
    - Color of paint or marker used
    - Messages in the graffiti
2. Look next for geographical information
    - Street (18th Street)
    - Neighborhood (Compton)
    - City (Los Angeles, etc.)
    - School (SMHS -- South Main High School -- Crips)
    - Zip code (01, 708, etc.)
    - Direction (East Side, West Side, South Side, etc.)
    - Geographic area (Downtown Mexicans; Uptown Crips; West Coast Cuzz, etc.)
    - Historical Landmark (Alamo Hustlers)
3. Isolate nicknames or monikers (street names)
    - These will be the names of the gang members or enemy members they have targeted
    - If just a few names are evident and not marked out, they usually wrote the graffiti
    - If many names are evident, it is a roll call
    - If names are marked out, those person have been targeted by the gang generating the graffiti

4. Isolate special messages
  - 187
    - Threat or brag of capital murder committed or to be committed
    - Names listed may be enemy gang members to be murdered
    - May also be names of those who planned or accomplished the murder
  - R.I.P.
    - Is a "roll call" of gang members killed or targeted by enemy gang
    - May be accompanied by threats to enemy gang
    - May have flower, masterpiece graffiti, other memorial, remembrances nearby
  - Indications of drugs for sale
    - Dollar signs
    - The word "CA$H"
    - The word "Stash"
    - A drawn eight-ball
    - Snowman
    - Snow White
    - THC
    - Marijuana leaf
    - 420
  - Any mention of weapons
    - CEG -- .357 Magnum
    - Deuce-e-deuce -- .22 pistol
    - Buckey -- shotgun
  - Actual or coded threats
    - "Five Popping, Six Dropping"
    - "Six High, Five Die"
    - "Wet 'Em Up"
    - "Let It Rain, Let It Flood, Let A Crip Kill A Blood"

- "FTW" – F—k the World
- "Where you from?"
- EGI – Everybody gets it
- AGI – Anybody gets it
- "Dissing" of other enemy gang's names or symbols
  - Enemy gang's symbols upside down
  - Enemy gang's symbols crossed out
  - Derisive comments and put-downs of enemy gangs
  - Taunts
  - Threats

14. Identifying Gangs By Their Characteristics

Hand Signs

Each street gang develops its own hand signs, a non-verbal system of communication used for identification and messaging or to challenge, insult, and show disrespect for other gangs and non-gang individuals, particularly law enforcement personnel.

The gang's own hand sign is made in the "up" position, and the enemy's hand sign is always thrown down as a gesture of disrespect. Gang hand signs are "flashed" or "stacked" quickly and changed as the need arises. While gangs sometimes incorporate American Sign Language hand and finger symbols into their gang hand signs, they are quite capable and innovative in creating their own.

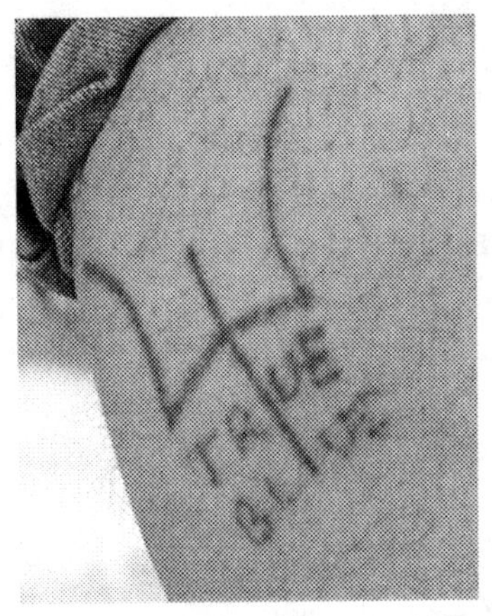

Tattoos

• Legal Restrictions on Professional Tattoo Parlors:

Tattoos (from the Tahitian word "tatu") have long been used to identify people in many cultures, including the gang culture of today.

Most states have laws regarding tattooing of the human body, and prohibit tattoo parlors from placing certain symbols on persons younger than 18 years of age without written consent from a parent or guardian who determines it to be in the best interest to cover a tattoo on the young person.

Covered by these laws are obscene tattoos, those that contain offensive language or symbols, gang-related names, symbols, or markings, drug-related names, symbols, or pictures, or some other type of words, symbols, or markings that a court considers would not be in the best interest of the minor to cover.

Gang members use tattoos to identify the gang and its members, and often such symbols are displayed prominently and visibly on the gang member's body in large, bold letters intended to intimidate other gang members and the community.

Tattoos often usually include one or more symbols, such as numbers, animals, crowns, pitchforks, eagles, and swords.

Former prison gang members may have a large number of tattoos. Wearing an unauthorized gang tattoo could be hazardous to a person's health, particularly in prison where non-gang members' unauthorized tattoos are sometimes cut from the flesh by angry gangbangers.

Some areas have grant programs that help defray the cost of removal or tattooing over gang tattoos.

Language, Mottos, Challenges

- People and Bloods
    - "Bloods Up, Crips Down"
    - "B's Up, C's Down"
    - BOS ("Beat on Sight")
    - "From Womb to Tomb"
    - "People Nation Left Side, West Side Best Side. Bloods Up!"
    - "All is All"
    - "All is Well"
    - "Always and Forever"
    - "Blood For Life"
    - "Five High, Six Die"
    - "Five Popping, Six Dropping"
    - "Five Pop, Six Drop."
    - "Let It Rain, Let It Drip, Let a Dawg Kill a Crip"
    - "My Crazy Life"
    - "S'up, Dawg?"
    - "What it B?"

- Folks and Crips
    - "Blue is True, Red is Dead"
    - "Crips Up, Bloods Down"

- "C's Up, B's Down"
- "ECC for Life" (East Coast)
- "S'up, Cuz?"
- "Lord, Lay Me Down to Sleep, With Six Dead Slobs at My Feet."
- "A Hustler Forever Grinds, A Diamond Forever Shines"
- "All is One"
- "Eye To Eye, We Never Die, We Just Multiply."
- "Folk Before Family"
- "Let it Rain, Let it Flood, Let a Crip Kill a Blood"
- "Life's a Gamble"
- "Stay True, Stay Clue"
- "True Clue 'Til I Die"
- "What it C?"
- "Six High, Five Die"
- "Six to the head, Five is dead"
- "Six is Flying, Five is Dying"
- "What's up, Mo?" (El Rukns, Blackstones)

- Gangster Disciples
  - "What it D?"
  - "S'up's up, G?"
  - "LLLKWU" (Love/Life/Loyalty/Knowledge/Wisdom/Understanding)
  - "What it G?"
  - "G's up, Hoes down."
  - "Six on Top, Can't be Stopped."
  - "When I Die, Show No Pity, Bury Me In Gangsta City, Brand 360 On My Chest, Tell the Folk I Did My Best"

Language and Slang

Gangs have a language unique to themselves and replete with criminal undertones. The glossary provided in this handbook can be used to translate conversations between and among gang members.

Gang terms learned in prison often indicate that an individual on the street has served time. Terms such as "boss" or "bas" are often required of prisoners and years of use are difficult to overcome. Other self-revealing terms, slang, or expressions often indicate previous incarceration.

One such is "tip up", which means to affiliate with or join a gang, as in, "Did you tip up?"

This term originated when illegal Hispanics previously incarcerated in an El Paso prison located at the "tip" of Texas reunited in the Huntsville Prison in Texas and formed the El Paso Tip gang. The initial use, as in the inquiry, "Are you tipped up?" asked if the new person was a member of the El Paso Tip gang. Eventually, it came to mean being associated with any gang in prison.

Other Identifiers

To show their affiliation with gangs, members will use and wear almost anything with distinctive marks and/or gang colors. These will often be worn or displayed "repping" to the right or left to indicate gang membership. Traditional colors, symbols, clothes, and other gang identifiers are changed whenever pressure is brought on gangs by law enforcement agencies, school officials, and parents.

- White tee shirts - favored by Hispanic gangs, usually sleeveless to show off tattoos and muscles; also Pendleton shirts
- Stocking caps - popular with Hispanic and Black gangs; with gang markings, gang symbols and names inside sweatband.
- Anklet, rubber bands - in gang colors on ankle, "repping" left or right
- Band-Aids - in gang colors, on right or left side
- Bandana - in gang colors; often with teardrops in the design; hanging from pocket, from belt loop, tied around leg, around arm, over shoulder, in hand, around head, repping to gang side; as scrunchies. (See gang colors chart in this Handbook.)

  - Folk and Crip
    - Blue and worn to the right
    - Often form a six-pointed star
  - People and Blood
    - Red and to the left
    - Designs often form a five-pointed star
- Bracelets
  - Plastic loops, shells, rubber bands, strings, other materials
  - In gang colors and worn "repping" to one side
  - With gang letter or symbol
- Beads, sometimes with names woven into belts
  - Black and gold - alternating 5 and 5, Latin Kings
    - 5 black and 5 gold - member
    - 2 black and 2 gold - Latin King executive members
    - All black - member of Assassins, Latin King enforcers
  - Black and green - 3 black and 3 green; 20 Luv

- Black and purple - no number pattern of beads; Jungle Brothers
- Black and white; black and red; maroon - Vice Lords
- Blue - Folk gangs; all blue beads indicate serious gangster
- Blue and white - Deuce Crips
- Blue, white, black - Folk gangs; multicolor beads alternating every six means moving up in rank; all multicolor means wearer has killed someone; blue and black indicate wearer is a gang leader; all black indicates a gang chief or retired gang chief
- Orange and white - Spanish Kings
- Purple and white - Latin Dragons
- Red - People, real gangster member
- Red and black – Bloods, People
- Red and blue - 3 red and 3 blue; Los Solidos
- Red, white, and black - People gangs; multicolor means wearer has killed someone; six alternating multicolors mean wearer is moving up in gang standing; red and black indicate you are one of the gang chiefs; black and white indicate a gang leader or retired gang leader
- Belt buckles
  - Often military type, usually metal
  - W/initial of gang on buckle, as "H" for Hoover Crips
  - Buckled to right or left on repping side
  - Long end hanging down on repping side
  - May be unbuckled to indicate readiness to fight; with long end hanging down on repping side
  - Buckle may be pulled noticeably to left or right to indicate which side the gang member "reps".

- Body
  - Use hands and fingers to form distinctive gang signs
  - "Repping" fold arms, lean body, tilt head, keep hand in pocket, bend knee, put foot forward, carry book bag -- either to right or left as per side gang "reps"
  - Slashed eyebrows - left or right, number and side show orientation of gang.
    - Right eyebrow - usually will be an even number -Folks
    - Left – usually will be an uneven number - People
    - MS 13 and some other Hispanic or Latino gangs will have one slash in right eyebrow and three in the left eyebrow
  - Pierced ears
    - 6 holes in right ear represent six-pointed star of David (Disciples)
    - 5 holes in left ear represents Vice Lords
  - Earring(s) "repping" to right or left
  - Teeth – one or more front teeth capped (sometimes gold) with gang sign etched or embedded; "grills" are often worn over front teeth with gang signs embedded
  - Fingernails - One or two nails painted with gang color(s) or symbols on right or left side, or nail pierced with small jewelry item indicating gang affiliation
  - Hair - shaved heads or extremely short hair are very popular with both Skinheads and certain Hispanic gangs; the latter often leave small ponytail or tuft of hair at the back of the neck.
    - Sideburns - extended by tattoo along lower jaw towards chin to form a crescent moon; is a Vice Lord indicator

- Streaked colors
  - Streaks total the number that is special to the gang (Example: Gangsters - 7)
  - On side gang is "repping"
    - Blue on right – Disciples
    - Gold or red on left – Vice Lords
- Combs or picks worn in front, back, right or left
- Designs cut in hair - pitchforks, initials, numbers
- Colored beads or barrettes in gang colors
  - Worn on specific "repping" side of head
  - Number of beads can indicate gang affiliation (Example: one bead - Corona De Rey)
  - Braided for belts or worn in hair, with colored beads spelling out the gang's name or the wearer's street name
  - Ponytail held by rubber bands of different colors, numbers
- Tattoos, branding, scarification
  - Gang symbols, numbers, or street names
    - Usually on side they are "repping"
    - May "dis" by displaying enemy gang's symbol
      - Upside down
      - Backwards
      - Crossed out
    - Cross on face
      - Wearer has killed a gang enemy
    - Teardrop on face - meaning varies by gang
      - Unshaded - has done a drive-by shooting

- Shaded - has killed an enemy gang member or one of his homies has been killed by enemy gang
- Buttons - in gang colors, w/gang initials, often in gang numbers
- Cap or hat, often sports team, often baseball cap, tilted to one side or worn backwards; often with writing on inside or lower brim. (Note: Color of the cap is not as important an identifier as is the side to which it is tilted. Also, the initial of the gang – such as C – takes preference over color).
    - Tilted right - Folks
    - Tilted left - People
    - Gangs often turn the bill to the back, with the cap strap on forehead; if in the middle, person may have no gang affiliation. Some gang members graffiti underneath the brim and flip the brim up so writing will show; some gang name on sweatband.
- Carry and play CDs and tapes
    - "Red" gang members (Bloods) will often have CDs in solid red cases with songs and rap putting down Crips
    - "Blue" gang members (Crips) will have these in solid blue cases with songs and rap putting down Bloods
- Combs
    - "Repping" to right or left, front or back
    - In gang colors
    - With gang initials or symbols
- Jewelry - shaped like stars, crowns, pyramids, dollars signs, initials, numbers, guns, marijuana leaf, cartoon characters..
- Bracelets - hand woven, in gang colors or with wearer's name

- Earrings
  - Worn in left or right ear only
  - In gang colors
  - With gang initial or symbol
- Gloves
  - Worn only on right or left hand as per gang orientation
    - Left hand - People, Vice Lords (VL often wear one white glove)
    - Right hand - Folk, Disciples
  - In gang colors
- Necklaces (called flats, bones, links, dukey ropes, bling)
  - Made of beads, jelly beads, shells, other materials in colors, numbers, or symbols indicating gang membership
    - Star of David is worn by Disciple Nation
    - Mariner Cross is worn by Disciple Nation
    - Joker's mask, sometimes red/blue - Los Solidos
- Other Jewelry - shaped like stars, crowns, pyramids, dollars signs, initials, numbers, guns, marijuana leaf, cartoon characters, and letter X for Malcolm X.
  - Bling refers to jewelry (from the sound it makes)
  - Bracelets - hand woven, in gang colors
  - 3 gold necklaces, each of different length, indicate Third World Disciple Nation gang
    - 1st is for "King" Larry Hoover Black Gangster Disciples
    - 2nd is for "King" David Barksdale (will have Star of David)
    - 3rd is for Jerome Freeman, Black Gangsters

- Heavy gold necklaces are a favorite of gang members; when worn with other gold jewelry is referred to as being "Turkish"
- New Wave Star – sheets of material worn under the hat or attached to the hat, hanging down the back, with gang colors
- Pants - worn in "L.A. sag" style, sagged below hips to expose buttocks.   Dickie brand pants are often worn by Hispanic gangs.
  - Pockets – inside dyed or sewn with gang colors
  - Pants legs
    - Right rolled up
      - Disciples
      - Simon City Royals
      - Folk
      - Crips
    - Left rolled up
      - Vice Lords
      - Latin Kings
      - People
      - Blood
  - Pants with crease pressed up to left or right
- Rings
  - Worn on right or left hand, worn on specific finger, with gang symbol
  - White ring or band worn on ring finger signifies wearer is a Brotherhood of the Struggle gang member who is a MOST – Member of Security Team; enforcer for the gang
  - Irish Friendship (Claddaugh), with crown – Latin Kings wear this because of the crown in the center
- Rubber bands – in gang colors; worn in hair, on wrist, on books, other items

- Sweatshirts or hoods of jackets exposed to show gang colors
- Shirts
    - Collar with one side turned up (repping), one side down or turned in
    - One sleeve rolled up, one rolled down
    - Shirt pulled out and hanging on one side to denote gang "repping"
    - Calvin Klein shirts worn by Bloods for CK initial; "Crip Killer"
- Team logos, colors, starter jackets, jogging suits, in team (gang) colors
- Shoes
    - Converse gym shoe - has five-pointed star and half crescent moon to one side; worn by Vice Lords.
    - British Knights - worn by Crips; BK for Blood Killer
    - Tongue - one laced (or only half-way up) up reveals gang's orientation, the other down (or half down) disses an enemy gang
        - Shoe laces
            - Color of shoe combined with color of laces in gang colors
            - Two sets of gang colored laces in both shoes;
            - Different gang colors in different shoes
            - Lacing or failing to lace certain holes in right or left shoe
            - Missing a certain eyelet to indicate gang number
                - People will lace only five holes
                - Folks will lace six
        - Laces arranged to form pattern or numbers

- In gang colors, w/gang laces, gang numbers (anything that can indicate gang numbers such as 5, 6, 7)
- Laced to indicate gang's initial(s) such as "C" or "B"

Numbers

0	- also 0-0, 0/0" double ought buck shot; also shotgun, "bucky"
01	- Blood
02	- 02 Bloods
001	- Blood love
006	- warning not to talk about gang business
013	- Blood code for "Attack him/them."
023	- Blood code for "Watch your back."
025	- Blood code for "What is your rank?"
031	- Blood code for "I am Blood."
041	- Blood code for "Kill the Crip."
1	- Amore De Rey (Love of the King; #1 = King, Christ, God); Latin Kings
2	- number used by Insane Deuces; often combined w/spear; sometimes 22
4	- Four Corner Hustlers
5	- People Nation gangs; Latin Kings use a five-pointed star
6	- Folk gangs, particularly Gangster Disciples; when upside down is dissing of Gangster Disciples' symbol
7	- 7th letter of alphabet "G"; gangster; sometimes used by 5 Per Centers to represent God
8	- (or eight-ball) – heroin (horse) for sale - announcement that drugs are for sale here, by this person; also refers to 1/8 ounce of cocaine; also refers to the alliance of Crips with the Folk Nation
9	- 9 mm handgun

10	- Mac 10 weapon; America's answer to the Israeli Uzi
11	- symbol of Vice Lords; also stands for Eleventh Street Posse; combinations of 11 are also used by KKK
13	- M, thirteenth letter of alphabet; number used by many Hispanic gangs; MS-13 (Mara Salvatrucha) Surenos, Mexican Mafia, Trece' (also called Tre)
14	- Norteno (Norte') gang number; also White Supremacist sign; stands for 14 racially-charged hate words spoken by white supremacist leader David Lane in a speech
16/12	- Hermanos de Pistoleroes Latinos
18	- 18th Street, also written XV3, 10VIII, and XVIII
20	- 20 Luv gang; Twenty to the Heart, 20 Luv, 20 Love
21	- stands for the 21 blocks in gang pyramid symbol, which are: 1. almighty 2. universe 3. mankind 4. religion 5, unity 6. search of self 7. great knowledge 8. non-violence 9. love of family 10. life 11. celebration 12. birth of self 13. love 14. truth 15. peace 16. freedom 17. justice 18. strength 19. power 20. loyalty 21. your word as your bond
2-2	- Border Brothers; also used by Insane Deuces and Two Two Boys
2-4	- stands for BD (Black Disciples); second and 4th letters of the alphabet;
2-6	- Two Sixers gang symbol; also written 2IV or 2-IV or with Roman numerals as IIV
2-7	- Black Guerrilla (Black Guerilla Family)
30	- Rolling Thirties gang symbol
40	- Rolling Forties gang symbol; also refers to a 40-ounce bottle of malt liquor
45	- Forty-Fives, offshoot gang of Hermanos de Pistoleros
50	- Rolling Fifties gang

59	- Five Nine Brims; also written Five 9 Brims and 5-9 Brims
60	- Rolling 60's gang
64	- 64 ounces of malt liquor
69	- motorcycle gang symbol; indicates wearer has been in prison or has committed sex crimes
86	- stop what you are doing; cease; abandon plan or action; from waitress lingo to cancel an order already placed
88	- white supremacist symbol; refers to eighth letter of alphabet to mean "Heil Hitler"
103	- stands for ten-three, 13th Street gang or 13 for Hispanic gangs
123	- first, second, and third letters of alphabet; ABC stands for Almighty Blue Crips
150	- Neta gang; also 1.50; means one hundred and fifty percent Neta
174	- denotes numbers of alphabet for IGD, Insane Gangster Disciples
183	- One Eight Trey Bloods
186	- Warning; be on lookout for someone trying to kill you
187	- California Penal Code for homocide
211	- police code for armed robbery
212	- indicates NY City area; Manhattan area code
213	- a Los Angeles area code used by some gangs, as 213 Crips
226	- police code for drugs
274	- numbers of the letters of the alphabet; BGD; Black Gangster Disciples
276	- numbers of the letters of the alphabet; BGF; Black Guerrilla Family)
311	- K is 11th letter of alphabet; stands for 3 K's, the KKK; also written 11-11-11 or 3K
312	- zip code of Chicago gangs, particularly Vice Lords
357	- .357 caliber handgun; also written CEG

360	- Folk Nation symbol; represents "Full Circle of Knowledge"; used by Black Gangster Disciples; their belief that Blacks once ruled the world and someday the world will go full circle (360 degrees) so will rule again; also can refer to a gang meeting or conference, a round table of 360 degrees; can refer to a circle around the six points of the Folk Nation Star of David symbol
360°	- refers to a "pure" or dedicated Black Gangster Disciple
406	- Gangster Disciple code for death violation
415	- area code of San Francisco, often used as a gang identifier by the Black Guerrilla Family and other gangs in that area, such as the 415 Crips
420	- marijuana; for sale; time to smoke marijuana also a number to designate Folks; also the anniversary of the Columbine school violence; also Hitler's birthday
440	- also written 440+; Black Souls
5150	- California code for involuntarily commitment for insane person
662	- MOB (Member of Bloods), spelled out on telephone dial
636	- F.O.L.K.$; often written backwards (reversed six, three, reversed six, 0 with a slash in the top, regular l, reversed K, and dollar sign)
666	- White supremacist symbol; also symbol of satanic cults, Aryan; also motorcycle gang symbol of Satan
666	- symbol of 18th Street Gang, (6+6+6 = 18)
720	- BGD's symbol for "3rd World Six Point Organization"; 360 X 2 = 720; twice as much knowledge as anybody else
808	- California penal code for disturbing the peace
911	- police; police are in the area; police are coming

1555	- The year the first slave ships arrived in America; number occasionally found in Black gang graffiti
5000	- goodbye; from "I'm outa (Audi 5000) here."
5150	- California Mental Health Code; refers to insane or vicious person
10III, XIII	- Sureno gang, Trece' gang, or may just refer to street or area code, as 13th Street Bloods and 02 Bloods; is sometimes used to signify marijuana or South Side

Combinations of Numbers, Words, Symbols

1%	- motorcycle gang term w/several different meanings - the AMA's claim that only 1% of all motorcycle riders in the country engage in criminal activity - some Harley riders claim that only 1% of all riders ride Harleys - 1960 motorcycle gangs' claim that "A One Percenter" is the 1% of a hundred of us (riders) who have given up on society and the politicians "one-way law." - the claim that 1% of motorcycle gangs members are members of the Outlaws and that 1% of motorcycle riders have Harley-Davidson machines
100%	- pure white or Anglo white pride symbol; white supremacist symbol
113% -	- 113% Sureno gang member
114%	- 114 % Norteno gang member
150%	- Neta; also written 1.50; 1 1/2;
1-1-15	- All is One
1-14-18	- BGDN for ADR (All Due Respect)
1	- BGDN for 1; One is All; also Islamic gangs for A (Allah)
2-G	- Black Gangsters (second letter of alphabet = 2); also Second Generation Gangster
2C	- Deuce Crips

2 HI	- Black P-Stone Nation and El Rukns; symbol or "two high" to signify they are too high (powerful) to be just street gangs
2-6	- Two Sixes Gang (Folks affiliated)
2-7-4-14	- BGDN, Black Gangster Disciple Nation; 2nd, 7th, 4th, and 14th letter
2-15-19	- BOS; second, fifth and nineteenth letters of the alphabet; BGD gang when incarcerated
2-15-19-19	- BOSS; Brothers of the Strong Struggle; second, fifth and nineteenth letters of the alphabet
2-15-20-19	- Brothers of the Struggle
3'CE	- Trece' Gang, Surenos
3-11	- 11th letter of alphabet is K; there are three 11's in 33: hence, KKK
4 pound	- forty-five caliber pistol
5 on it	- five dollar buy of marijuana
5X2	- Five Deuce gang
5-33	- KKK; K is 11th letter of alphabet; there are three 11's in 33; the 5 stands for the current or fifth era of the KKK
5-plated	- nickel plated handgun
6 Alive	- Spanish Cobras (six refers to the six letters in Cobras)
7-4	- Gangster Disciples
8; 8-3	- Hoovers; Hoover Crips
10	- BDG for j (Justice)
10-3; 10III	- also 10 3; stands for 13; Sureno gangs claim 13; also Mexican Mafia and other Hispanic and Latino gangs
11	- BGD for K (Knowledge)
11-11-11	- KKK; also written XI-XI-XI
12-12-12.	- L is the 12th letter of alphabet; stands for Life, Liberty, Loyalty; is also written LLL
12-20-20-3	- BDG for Love To The Club
13, 10-3	- 13 can also be shown as 3'CE and 3 dots over a horizontal bar; also stands for marijuana; symbol indicates person selling marijuana or other drugs; can refer to selling

	meth; also a symbol of many Hispanic gangs
13 ½; 13.5	- gang's cynical view of justice in a criminal trial; thirteen people -12 jurors and one judge, who is called a "half -ass judge"; also written 13.5
14; 10-4; X4	- Norteno gangs claim 14; Catorce gang; also ENE gang; can also be written 4'CE; also stands for Nation
16-12	- 16th and 12th letters of the alphabet, used by Pistoleros Latinos, an HPL gang.
23-24	- prison; refers to 23 out of 24 hours in cell each day
24-7	- constantly, 24 hours each day, seven days a week; also refers to prison
25L	- twenty-five years to live prison sentence
50-50	- neutral individual; non-gang member; no gang affiliation
100	- one hundred proof; the real thing; knowledge; full circle of knowledge

Roman Numerals

I	- Latin Kings; Corona Del Rey symbol; Number One; Christ is King; Crown of the King
II; 2C	- Duece Crips symbol
III	- TRE' (Trecé) gang
X3; XIII; 10III	- 13; used by many Hispanic gangs; Surenos, Mexican Mafia, Mara Salvatrucha gang from El Salvador; can also stand for ZIP code of gang or marijuana
V	- Blood and People symbol
VI	- Crip and Folk symbol
XI-XI-XI	- KKK
XIII	- M; many Hispanic Gangs
XIV, 1014	- symbol for 14, Norteno gang; Catorce' gang

Colors - Quick Reference

As soon as gangs become aware that the authorities know their colors, they will switch to alternative colors or plaids. While still popular as a gang identifier, colors by themselves are *the least reliable gang identifier of gang membership and therefore should be considered as supporting documentation in concert with other identifiers*

Colors	Gang
Aqua, White	Crazy Brotherhood Clan
Beige (Light), White	Together We Kill
Black	Braziers, Gaylords Ghetto Brothers Insane Dragons, Latin Dragons
Black, Blue	Black Gangster Disciples Black Souls Disciples Folk Nation Gangster Disciples Insane Popes Latin Disciples Maniac Latin Disciples Ridgeway Lords Simon City Royals Spanish Cobras Two-Two Boys Unknown Assassins
Black, Blue (Baby or Light)	Ambrose Disciples Spanish Gangster Spanish Gangster Disciples Young Latino Organization
Black, Blue, White	Insane Popes Six Thirty Six (636) Folks
Black, Brown	Latin Jivers
Black, Brown, Yellow	Orchestra Albany
Black, Gold (Yellow)	Arab Posse Eleventh Street Posse Four Corner Hustlers Latin Kings TAP Boys

Black, Green	Aztecs
	Insane Deuces
	La Primera
	Spanish Cobras
Black, Green (Forest), Yellow	Asian Boys
Black, Gray	Boyz in the Hood
	Gaylords
	Latin Eagles
	New Breed
Black, Khaki	Latin Dragons
	Sane
Black, Maroon	Latin Souls
	Party Gents
Black, Pink	Imperial Gangsters
Black, Purple	Tiny Rascal Gangsters
Black, Red	Black P-Stones
	Cobrastones
	Four Corner Hustlers
	Insane Latin Hustlers
	Latin Counts
	Mickey Cobras
	People Nation
	Stone Freaks
	Vice Lords
Black, Tan	Two-Sixers
Black, White	Almighty Players
	Brothers (Brothas)
	Home Boys
	Park Boys
	Party People
	Untouchable Vice Lords
	Warlords
	Four Corner Hustlers
Black, Yellow	Satan's Disciples
	Vice Lords
Blue	Crips
	Mara Salvatrucha
	Oriental Street Boyz
Blue (Dark Regal), White	True Down Veteranos
Blue, Gray (sometimes)	Tiny Rascals
Blue, Red	Los Solidos

Color	Gang
Blue, Red, White	Mara Salvatrucha (Leaders - black bandanas) Neta
Brown	Los Cholos
Brown, Tan	Brown Pride Locos
Gray	Aerosol Bombing Crew
Gray, Green	Fast Tagging Styles
Gray, Maroon	Fearless Bombing Assassins Free Breaking Artists
Green (Lime) and White	Krazy Ass Kriminals
Green, Red, White	C $ Notes La Raza Mexican Mafia
Green, White	Kriminals
Maroon	Outlawz
Orange	Future Stones
Purple	Grape Crips Grape Mafia Crips Grape Street Crips Kriminals of Art
Red	Bloods Blood Red Dragons (Asian)
Red, Yellow	Latin Lovers

Logos and Sports Team Clothing Quick Reference

TEAM	GANG	ASSOCIATION
Atlanta Braves	People	"Almighty" People
Boston Celtics	Spanish Cobras	"C" and colors
California Angels	People, Latin Saints, Orchestra Albany	The "A" and/or the colors; Latin Saints' symbol is halo above an "A"
Charlotte Hornets	4 Corner Hustlers, Imperial Gangsters	"CH"; Colors

Chicago Blackhawks	Vice Lords	Colors
Chicago Bulls	People, Bloods, Vice Lords, Latin Counts, Latin Lovers (BULLs), Mickey Cobras, Black P-Stone	Colors, horns on bull form forks up, are Disciple symbol; "Bloods Usually Live Longer, Sucker", "Boy, You Look Like Stone"
Chicago Cubs	Spanish Cobras	"C"
Chicago White Sox	Crips	"X" for "X Out Slobs"
Cincinnati Reds	People, Cobra Stones, Latin Counts	"C" for Cobra Stones, Latin Counts
Colorado Rockies	Crips; Simon City Royals	"SC" for Simon City; "CR" for "Crips Rule"
Dallas Cowboys	People, Crips	"C", 5-point star; "Crips On Wheels Banging On You Slobs"
Denver Broncos	Black Disciples	"DB" reversed is BD; colors
Detroit Lions	Black Gangster Disciples	Colors
Detroit Tigers	Folks, Latin Disciples, Gangster Disciples, Maniac Latin Disciples, Satan's Disciples	"D"; colors
Duke Blue Devils	Folks	Devil has horns, upside crown in hand (dissing Kings)

Duke University	Folks, Disciples	"D"; logo devil holds upward pitchfork; "Disciples Utilizing Knowledge Everyday", "Disciples Usually Kill Everyone"
Florida Marlins	Folks	"F" initials
Georgetown Hoyas	Folks, Hoover Crips, Gangster Disciples	"Hoovers On Your Ass, Slob"; "G", hat on bulldog "reps" to the right, six studs on the collar
Georgia Tech	Folks, Gangster Disciples	"G"
Green Bay Packers	Gangster Disciples	"G" symbol
Houston Astros	Folks, Hoover Crips	"H" over star, "High Five"
Indiana University	Folks	"I" and "U" logo resemble pitchfork up
Kansas City Chiefs	Folks, Bloods, Piru, Latin Lovers	Colors, KC for "Kill Crips"; "Crips Hated In Each F--king State"; "Kill All Nigga Suck Ass Slobs"
Kansas City Royals	King Cobras, Simon City Royals	"KC" for King Cobras; "R" for Simon City Royals
Los Angeles Dodgers	Disciples	"D"

Los Angeles Kings	People, Latin Kings	"Kings"; "Kill Inglewood Nasty Gangsters"; "Kill Innocent Niggaz Gangsta Style"
Los Angeles Lakers	Crips, Grape Street sets	No known acronym
Los Angeles Raiders	People, Brothers of the Struggles, Gangster Disciples (blue and black colors), Maniac Latin Disciples	Colors, initials such as "Ruthless Ass Insane Disciples Running S--t" or "Raggedy Ass Iced Doughnuts Everywhere Running Scared"
Miami Hurricanes	Crips, Hoover sets	"MH"; Magnificent Hoovers
Michigan Wolverines	Maniac Latin Disciples	"M"
Minnesota Northstars	Maniac Latin Disciples	"M"
Minnesota Twins	Maniac Latin Disciples	"M"
New Orleans Saints	Folks, Crips	"Slobs Ain't S--t"; colors
New York Giants	Folks, Crips	"Going Insane All Night Toward Slobs"; "Giant Instant Niggaz Terminate Slobs"
New York Yankees	Gangster Disciples	Colors
North Carolina College	Folks, Crips, Cobras	"N" and "C"

North Carolina Tar Heels	Neighborhood Crips	"NC"; colors
Notre Dame	Disciple Nation	"ND" reversed is "DN"
Oakland A's	Ambrose, Orchestra Albany; Spanish Cobras	"A"; colors
Oakland Raiders	People	5-point star symbol; "Remember After I Die Everybody Runs Scared"; "Ruthless and Insane Disciples Eliminating Red Slobs"; "Raggedy Assed Iced Doughnuts Running Scared"; "Ruthless Ass Insane Disciples Everywhere Running S--t:
Orlando Magic	People; Maniac Latin Disciples	5-point star on jacket; "Murder All Gangsters In the City"; "Maniacs (MLD) and Gangsters in Chicago"
Philadelphia Phillies	People, Bloods	"P"; colors
Philadelphia Stars	People	"P"; 5-point star

Phoenix Suns	Black P-Stone Nation	"PS"
Pittsburgh Pirates	People, Bloods, Pirus, Latin Kings	"P" and Colors
San Antonio Spurs	People, Bloods	Colors
San Diego Padres	Folks, Satan Disciples	"SD"
San Francisco (Any Team)	Stone Freaks	"FS"
San Francisco Giants	Folks, Future Stones	Initials switched stand for "Super Gangster Folk" or "Future Stones"
Seattle Mariners	Crips, Rolling Sixties	"S" for Sixties; "Murder all Roo (Piru) Idiots Now, Eliminate Red Slobs"
St. Louis Cardinals	Spanish Vice Lords	Hat predominately red
Tampa Bay Lightning	Gangster Disciples	Colors
Texas Rangers	People	Initials form pitchfork down
University of Illinois	Folks	Initials form pitchfork up
University of Indiana	Imperial Gangsters	Initials form pitchfork up
University of Texas	Insane Folk	Initials form heart with horns emerging; also form pitchfork up

| UNLV | Disciples; Vice Lords; Nortenos; Northern Structure | "Us (Nigga's/Nortenos) Live Viciously"; "Us Nigga/Nortenos) Love Violence"; initials backwards for "Vice Lords Nation United" |

Symbols - Quick Reference

Gangs change and add to their symbols to confuse the authorities and enemy gangs.

- Arrows, directional
    - ↓ - Downtown or Southside, as in M↓ = Downtown Mexicans
    - → - Eastside, as in Eastside Mexicans
    - ← - Westside, as in Westside Mexicans
    - ↑ - Uptown or Northside, as in Uptown Mexicans
- A, scripted - Ambrose gang; often shown with plumed hat
- A - with "O" drawn around it, crossbar on lower circle area; Orchestra Albany
- Asterisk, modified - perpendicular line of cross shortened, rays radiating out, looks like an asterisk; Hispanic gang
- B, scripted - Bishops gang; usually in Gothic, often with Bishop's cross
- Bishop's miter and cross - symbol of Bishops gang
- Bows - symbol of Brothers of White Strength
- Bulldog head w/crown - symbol of Latin Kings gang; studs on dog's collar signifies gang's orientation

- Bunny head, both ears straight up - Vice Lords, Party People symbol
- Bunny head, upside down - dissing of Party People, Playboys, Vice Lords
- Bunny head, w/forward ear bent - symbol of Folk gang; also Simon City Royals, often with SCR; symbol of Latin Kings
- Bunny head, often with fedora, sunglasses, forward ear bent, dice with 2 and 6 showing - Two Sixers Nation
- Card w/2 of spades - symbol of Insane Deuces and sometimes Deuce Crips
- Cane, party - symbol of Vice Lords, Party Gents, Playboys
- Cane, upside down – dissing of party cane gangs
- CA$H – Symbol often used by Cash Flow Posse; also is used by other gangs signifying drugs for sale; also used by Skinhead white supremacist gang Chicago Area Skin Heads
- Cell (prison) window with sun or bird showing through bars - has done prison time; signifies waiting to be released
- CG - rank in Gangsta gangs; Captain of Gangstas
- Chains, sometimes broken - NETA
- Champagne or martini glass - symbol of People gangs; Vice Lords
- Circle, w/cross - symbols of white power supremacists groups
- Clock face without hands - doing prison time

- Clock, w/hands at 10 and 4 - stands for 14;
  number used by Norteno gangs,
  also called Catorce
- Coat of armor - symbol of Latin Kings
- Cobra - snake curved in form of an S, tongue
  and/or tail are raised pitchforks; usually clearly a
  cobra; often has SC; Spanish Cobras
- Crescent, or half moon - symbol of People
  gangs
- Cresent, with five-pointed star - Vice Lords
- Cross, Celtic - symbol used by many white racist
  gangs
- Cross, Catholic - Latin Gangs
- Cross, Pachuco - Hispanic gang; has rays
  radiating outward
- Cross, Spanish - symbol of People gangs;
  Spanish Gangsters, Spanish Cobras
- Cross, with red blood drop in center - Ku Klux
  Klan
- Cross, Spanish w/2 dots & 3 lines on top -
  United Latin Organization
- Cross w/halo and 3 lines; hooded figure with
  cross - Insane Popes
- Cross w/rays and "P" - Pachucos; also use
  same symbol as Cholos gang, which is a
  gangster face with a hat, dark glasses, drooping
  mustache, long goatee
- Cross, with circle of dots - Latin Souls; LS
- Crown, w/3 or w/5 sharp points - Latin Kings and
  some other People-related gangs; the 5 points
  stand for Love, Truth, Peace, Freedom, Justice
- Crown, w/6 points - Crown, w/six _rounded_ points
  - Folk-affiliated gangs; points often "rounded"
- Crown w/rounded edges - Imperial Gangsters,
  often with initials IG and raised pitchfork

- Crown, cut in half - dissing of People gang symbol
- "D" w/backward swastika inside - Disciples symbol
- Devil, w/pitchfork - Satan's disciples; also called Devil's Disciples
- Devil's tail - Folks symbol; w/heart it is symbol of Latin Disciples
- Deuce (2) - often combined with gang initials as in 5D, as in 5X2 + Five Deuce gang
- Diamond, w/5 points - symbol of Future Stones, Vice Lords, Cobras
- Dice, one or two, w/number 2 showing - Insane Deuces
- Dice, two w/number 2 on both - symbol of Two Two Boys
- Dice, two w/number 3 on both - symbol of the Two Sixers gang
- Dice, one w/number 5 showing - symbol of a Peoples gang
- Dice, one w/ number 6 showing - symbol of a Folks gang
- Dice, w/2 on one side and 6 on other side - Two Sixers
- Dog(s), faces of - Bloods call themselves "Dawgs"; dog faces sometimes used in their graffiti
- Dollar sign - power, money, drugs; used by gangs to denote selling of drugs; also used by Cash Flow Posse and 4 Korner Hustlers as part of their gang symbols; often found in GD and Blood graffiti as "WHAT'$ UP?"
- Dots, three - Three dots (two over one); represents a dog's paw; Bloods call themselves "dogs"; these three dots also stand for "My Crazy Life"

- Dots, 3 around top of a cross or above the tines up upturned pitchfork - Folk gang symbol
- Dot, one over pitchfork up, or over a "t" - stands for True Crip
- Dots, five - Latin Kings;
- Dots, five on web of hand by thumb - Asian gang symbol
- Dragon - Insane Dragons
- Dragon, Red - Red Blood Dragons
- Dragon, Chinese, with prison tower - Black Guerilla Family
- Eagle - symbol of Latin Eagles, Asian Black Eagles gang
- Eagle, on cactus, clutching snake - often includes Mexican flag; symbol of Latin Eagles, Mexican Mafia, and Mi Raza Unida and sometimes Spanish Eagles
- Eagle w/snake and M - symbol of Mexikanemi
- Eagle w/AB - symbol of American Breed, a motorcycle gang; often uses Anheuser Busch logo in graffiti
- Eagle, holding snake, sitting on cactus - symbol of EME (Mexican Mafia; also called Mexican Mafia); Eye, of Allah - all-seeing eye, symbol used in Vice Lord, other People gangs
- "Better Guidance" - Black Gangstas
- Eight ball - a measure of cocaine; symbol indicates gang is selling drugs; is also a prison symbol for bad luck; also is symbol of Eight Ball Posse gang
- Face, female crying - prison tattoo; someone is waiting for prisoner's release
- Face, sad or mean - Brothers of the Struggle, Brothers of Sorrow
- Faces, one laughing, one crying - Play now, pay later; my happy, now sad life

- Featherwood - White pride female gang tattoo
- Fist, white and clenched - White power sign of white supremacists and motorcycle gangs
- Fist, black and clenched - Black Guerrilla Family
- Flag, Puerto Rico - NETA (often shows two Puerto Rican flags, crossed)
- Glove - symbol of People gangs
- Halo - Latin Saints
- Hand, shackled, chained - NETA; usually hand has middle finger crossed over index finger; thumb and other fingers are usually turned in to palm, thumb atop
- Face, round w/mean or sad look - Brotherhood of Struggle
- Face - w/hat, dark sunglasses, drooping mustache, long pointed beard - is symbol of both the Cholos and the Pachucos gangs
- Face, hooded - symbol of Maniac Latin Disciples; also may be a hooded figure
- Hand, black - symbol of Mexican Mafia; often has "EME", "M", or "MM" in palm of hand
- Hands, chained over a rifle and a sword crossed - Black Guerilla Family
- Headdress, feathered - Hells Angels (motorcycle gang)
- Heart - Folks symbol
- Heart w/cross - symbol of Spanish Lords, sometimes w/crown
- Heart w/horns - Spanish Gangsters
- Heart w/horns on top & devil's tail below, swastika, raised pitchfork, letters LD or MLD - Latin Disciples or Maniac Latin Disciples
- Heart w/wings - Latin Lover; may have pitchfork up, LL

- Heart w/wings - is Black Gangster Disciple if combined with BGD, six-pointed star, upwards pitchfork
- Helmet, knights - Latin Count, usually includes initials LC
- Helmet, plumed w/spear - Ambrose (usually includes an A)
- Helmet, plumed - Hell's Angels (motorcycle gang)
- Helmet, Roman - symbol of Latin Brothers Nation, usually has LBN
- Hispanic Cross - also called Pachuco cross; worn by Pachuco gang members during the 1940's; often found on web of hand near thumb.
- Hooded face or figure - symbol of Maniac Latin Disciples
- Horns, devil's - Folks symbol
- Horns, on helmet - Hell's Angels (motorcycle gang)
- K or K-Town - gang associated with Two Sixers
- King's head - Mexican Kings
- King's head w/crown - Latin Kings
- "Life's a Gamble" - Folk motto, often shown with one dice showing a number 6
- Lightning bolt - White supremacist symbol; Aryan Brotherhood of Texas symbol
- LLL - stands for Love, Life, Liberty; 12th number of the alphabet; also written 12.12.12.; Black Gangster Disciples
- LTPFJ - stands for 5 points of star; Love, Truth, Peace, Freedom, Justice; often used by Latin Kings
- Lion's head w/crown - symbol of Latin Kings
- M - Mexican Mafia; also called EME
- MM - Mexican Mafia; also called EME

- Map of Africa - Zulu Nation
- Machetes, crossed, w/shield and or eagle - Mexican Mafia
- Map of Vietnam - Vietnamese gang tattoo
- Masks, Theater Sad/Happy - Los Solidos
- Masonic symbol - used by Gangster Disciples
- Mexican Flag - symbol of La Raza
- Mexican War God - symbol of Mexican Mafia
- Mickey Mouse - Mexican Mafia
- MOB - Member of Bloods, spelled out on telephone dial
- Moon, crescent - El Rukns; often shown with five-pointed star, eye, sword, numeral 7
- Moons, two half-crescent - Cobra Stones, Mickey Cobras; often shown with five-pointed star, pyramid, eye
- MOST - Brotherhood of Struggle term for Members of Security Team
- O - usually superimposed with an "A"; Orchestra Albany
- One Hundred Percent Wood - pure Peckerwood, white power gang
- One Percenter - Refers either to the 1% of all motorcycle riders being involved in criminal activity, or to the 1% of all motorcycle riders who ride Harleys
- Pachuco Cross - also called Hispanic Cross, see above
- Panther - Imperial Gangsters; often shown with crown with rounded edges, pitchfork up, and IG initials
- Peckerwood - White pride gang tattoo
- Pitchfork, points up ψ - gang is affiliated with Folks

- Pitchfork, points down - gang is affiliated with People
- Pitchfork upright between "L" and "O" (LTO) -- Latins Taking Over
- Plumed hat, with scripted "A" - Ambrose gang
- Prison, being attacked by a dragon - Black Guerilla Family
- Prison walls - Has done prison time
- Prison walls, falling outward - waiting to get out of prison
- Pure Wood - true Peckerwood, white power gang
- Pyramid - symbol of People gangs; w/21 bricks, is symbol of Future Stones gang; with PS is symbol of Puerto Rican Stones
- Pyramid w/staff - Vice Lords
- Pyramid w/crescent moon - El Rukn symbol; claim pyramids built by Black engineers; crescent represents Blacks split into two parts of world
- Rabbit head, w/bent ear is a Folk sign; straight ear, is People
- Real Wood - pure Peckerwood, white power gang
- RIP - "Roll call"; usually graffiti listing names of dead gang members
- Rosary, Catholic - Latin gangs
- Shield w/shamrock or swastika - white supremacist symbol, often with rays or lightning bolts emanating
- Shield, w/crossed spears behind and sword below - Mandingo Warriors
- Shield w/ two lions - Two-Two Boys
- Shield, w/two feathers - Warrior Society

- Snake, feathered,, sometimes with Mexican eagle - symbol of Mexikanemi, often called the "Texas Mexican Mafia"
- Skull, or skull w/devil's horns - Hell's Angels (motorcycle gang)
- Skull, with MM, sometimes w/wings - "Old" Mexican Mafia
- Skull w/crossed pistols - Outlaws (motorcycle gang)
- Snake, curves form an "M" - Mexikanemi gang symbol; may include eagle
- Sombrero, covering machete dripping blood or with machete dripping blood stabbed through the sombrero - Nuestra Familia
- Souls - Latin Souls
- Spider or cobwebs - has done or is doing prison time
- SS - White supremacist symbol (Nazi Storm Trooper symbol)
- ST or S/T - Syndicato Tejas, or Texas Syndicate
- Staff, shepherd's crook - symbol of People's gangs
- Stars - several anywhere on body denotes Nuestra Familia member who is a killer for the gang
- Star, on forehead - Nuestra Familia member who has killed for gang
- Star, w/3 or 5 _sharp_ points - Latin Kings, People
- Star, 5 points, cut or broken in half - dissing of People 5 pointed star
- Star, w/5 points, blue - Nuestra Familia
- Star, w/5 points, w/TS or ST and/or outline of State of Texas - Texas Syndicate

- Star, w/6 _rounded_ points - Folk-affiliated gangs; 6 points stand for Love, Unity, Money, Loyalty, Wisdom, Understanding (LUMLUW)
- Star, 6 points, w/upward pitchfork - symbol of Black Disciples
- Star, w/rays radiating out - often called "Hispanic" or "Spanish" star; People-affiliated gangs, particularly Latin Kings
- Stickman figure w/halo, sometimes w/staff - Latin Saints
- Swastika - white supremacist symbol
- Swastika, backwards - symbol of Folk gang; often used by Hispanic gangs, especially the Latin Eagles, in memory of David "Hitler" Ramirez whose gang adopted it as their symbol
- Swastika, alone or w/three-leaf clover - Aryan Brotherhood; can also include AB, 666, SWP (Supreme White Power), 100% Pure, Peckerwood, and/or picture of a butterfly
- Swastika, enclosed in circle; symbol of NSWPP
- Sword - Folk-affiliated gangs; also symbol of some white supremacist groups
- Sword, crossed with rifle - Black Guerrilla Family
- Swords, two crossed, w/"G" - Grandel gang, mostly Hispanic
- Swords, two, encircling a "G" - Grandel gang
- Teardrops - any gang; tattooed on side gang reps; each silhouette of teardrop signifies fellow gang member killed by enemy; each teardrop completely inked indicates one enemy gang member killed by wearer
- Te Ese - Texas Syndicate
- Tombstones with numbers - number of years has done prison time
- Tombstones with numbers and RIP - friends who have been killed

- Top Hat and Cane - Party Gents
- Top Hat, cane, and glove(s) - Vice Lords
- Top Hat upside down - dissing of top hat gang symbol
- TS or T/S - Texas Syndicate
- Triangle, w/broken four-sided triangle superimposed to form letters "GD" - Gangster Disciples
- Triangle, w/dot at each point and an "F" beneath the triangle - Cash Flow Family
- Viking - white power tattoo
- White Power - symbol of KKK
- Wings, pin - when worn by a motorcycle gang member, means he is a "One-Percenter"
- Wreath, with cross - Gaylords
- $ - used in place of letter s or z; also means money and power
- $ - also indicates gang is selling drugs, as in Ea$t Coa$t Cu$$
- $ - also is symbol of Vice Lords

Gangs and Symbols They Use

Action Pack Gangsters	Folks	Initials "APG"; "Folks" & BGD logo
Akrhos (Kings)	People	Latin Kings & "People" logo
Albanian Gangsters	None	Initials "A" & "G"
Ambrose	Folks	Script initial "A"; plumed helmet w/ spear
American Breed	Motorcyc le	Name "American Breed"; Anheuser Busch Logo; initial "A" w/ eagle flying through
Angels of Death	Devil Worship pers	Satan drawings; initials "AOD"
Anti-White Power Skinheads	Anti- White Suprema cists	Initials "WPK" ("White Power Killers")

Gang	Affiliation	Identifiers
Arab Posse	People	Five-pointed star; initials "TAP"; "People" logo
Aryan Brotherhood	Prison	Swastika; initials "AB"; 666; SS lightning bolts
Aryan Nation	Prison	Shield w/ shamrock or swastika
Ashland Vikings	Folks	Viking helmet; six-pointed star
Assyrian Eagles	People	Eagle; initials "AE"
Avers Boys Organization	None	Initials "ABO"
Aztec Nation	People	Initials "AN"; "People" logo
Bassheads	People	Cross w/ one dot in each corner
Be-Be	People	"People" and Latin Kings logos; word "Be-Be"
Bishops	People	Gothic initial "B"; Bishop's miter & cross
Black Disciples	Folks	Six-pointed star; upward crossed pitchforks
Black Eagles	Asian	Eagle
Black Gangster Disciples	Folks	The BGDs, GDs, and BOS use pitchforks up and the six-pointed star
Black Mafia	Prison	Initials "BM"; crossed rifle and sword
Black Peace Stone Nation	People	Crescent moon; five-pointed star; pyramid w/ five-pointed star
Black Souls 440+	Folks	"Folks" logo
Boys in the Hood	People	Initials "BH"; "People" logo
Brothers of the Struggle	Prison	Incarcerated members of the BGDs
C-Notes	Folks	Dollar sign - $; "Folks" logo
Campbell Boys	Folks	Devil's horns; upraised pitchforks
Channel One Posse	Jamaican	Narcotics trafficking/sales
Chicano Cholos	Folks	Initials "CC"; upward pitchforks; "Folks" logo
Crips	Folks	Originated Los Angeles, CA
Cullerton Deuces	People	Spade cards w/2; dice showing 2
DC Eagles	Motorcycle	Name "DC Eagles"; eagle head

Gang	Alliance	Symbols
East Side Homeboys	People	VL logos; cross; "People" logo
Eight Ball Posse	None	Eight ball; initials "EBP"
El Rukns	People	Crescent moon w/ five-pointed star; pyramid w/ crescent moon; number 7 inside a circle
11th Street Posse	People	"People" logo; VL logo
Flying Dragons	Asian	None
Future Stones	People	Five-pointed diamond; pyramid w/ 21 bricks; initials "FS"; Number 5
Gaylords	People	Cross w/ wreath; initials "GL"
Ghost Shadow	Asian	None
Harrison Gents	Folks	Two crossed canes w/ top hat and initials "HG"
Hell's Angels	Motorcycle	Name "Hell's Angels"; skull w/devil horns, helmet & feathered head dress
Hell's Henchmen	Motorcycle	Name "Hell's Henchmen"; hooded skull
Imperial Gangters	Folks	Rounded crown; pitchfork; pink panther; initials "IG"
Insane Deuces	People	Playing card w/ 2 of spades; dice showing 2; 2 w/ spear
Insane Popes	Folks	Cloaked or hooded figure w/ cross
Insane Unknowns	People	White robed figure w/ rifle; cross w/ initials "UNKNS"
Italian Playboys	None	Playboy bunny; initials "IPB"
Jousters	People	Knight's head; backward swastika; initials "TJN"; "People" logo
Kents	People	Words "Kent", "You Feel It" along with "People" logo
KGB	Unknown	Initials "KGB" (Krazy Get Down Boys)
Ku Klux Klan	None	Initials "KKK"; words "White Power"
La Primera	People	Initials "LP"; "People" logo
La Raza	Folks	Mexican flag or eagle; initials "LRZ"; "Folks" logo
Laos Posse	Folks	Initials "LP"; "Folks" logo

Latin Brothers	People	Roman warrior helmet; initials "LBN"
Latin Counts	People	Knight's helmet; initials "LC"
Latin Disciples	None	Heart w/ Devil's tail & horns; pitchfork; initials "MLD" or "FMLDN"; initial "D" w/ backward swastika inside
Latin Dragons	Folks	Fire breathing dragon; six-pointed star
Latin Eagles	Folks	Eagle head or eagle in flight
Latin Family	Prison/Folks	Consists of Latin "Folk" gang members
Latin Homeboys	People	Cross; closed fists
Latin Jivers	Folks	Initials "LJ"; pitchforks
Latin Kings	People	Three- or five-pointed crown; five-pointed star; five dots; cross; king's head w/ crown
Latin Locos	Folks	"Folks" logo; Two Sixers logo; initials "LL"
Latin Lovers	Folks	Heart w/ wings; pitchforks up
Latin Saints	People	Stickman figure w/ halo above it
Latin Souls	Folks	Initials "LS" w/ cross
Latin Stones	People	"People" and VL logos
Latin Youth	Folks	Initials "LYZ"; "Folks" logo
Loco Boys	None	Initials "LB"
Majestic Party Crew	People	Initials "MPC"; "People" logo
Mexican Kings	People	Five-pointed star; king's head
Mickey Cobras	People	Cobra; initials "MC"; "People" logo
Milwaukee Kings	People	Same as Latin Kings
New Breed-LLL	Folks	Initials "NB"; "BG" (Better Guidance/Black Gangster); "LLL" (Love, Life & Loyalty)
Noble Knights	People	Roman knight head w/ plume
North Siders	Prison	Nazi symbolism; initials "NS"
Orchestra Albany	Folks	Initials "OA"
Motorcycle Outlaws	Motorcycle	Name "Outlaws"; skull w/ crossed pistons

Pachucos	People	Rayed cross and initial "P"; gangster w/ dark glasses, hat & goatee
Park Boys	People	"People" logo; initials "PB"
Party People	Folks	Playboy bunny; initials "pp"
Piper Lane Lovers	Folks	"Folks" logo
PR Stones	People	Pyramid; "People" logo; words "PR Stones"
Ridgeway Lords	Folks	Initials "RL"; "Folks" logo
Satan Disciples	Folks	Pitchfork; devil; "Folks" logo
Scorpions	Asian	Scorpion
Simon City Royals	Folks	Rabbit head w/ bent ear; cross hat w/crossed shotguns; initials "SCR"
Southern Illinois Association	Prison	"Nazi" and "White Power" Symbolism (breakaway group of Northside gang
Spanish Cobras	Folks	King cobra snake; initials "SC", "ISC"
Spanish Gangsters	Folks	Six-pointed star; heart w/ horn
Spanish Lords	People	Heart w/ cross; crown; initials "SL"
Stone Freaks	None	Initials "SF"
II Down Posse	People	Words "II Down"
12th Street Players	People	Initials "TPN"; upward pitchforks
Two Sixers	Folks	Playboy bunny w/ fedora, bent ear, & glasses; pair of dice w/ tattoos w/ 3 dots
Two-Two Boys	Folks	Two dice showing 2; crest or shield w/ two lions
Unknown Assassins	Folks	Initials "UA"; "Folks" logo
Vice Lords	People	Pyramid w/ crescent moon; initials "VL"; top hat w/cane and gloves; pair of dice; martini glass; playboy bunny head; crescent moon w/five-pointed star; dollar sign
Warlords	People	Initials "WL"; "People" logo
West Side Homeboys	Folks	"Folks" & Imperial Gangsters logos

Vocabulary of Drugs, Gangs, and the Street

A

ABG - "Anybody gets it"; warning of random gang violence

ACAB - skinhead acronym for "All Cops Are Bastards"

academy - jail, prison

ace cool - best friend, backup in gang activities

ADR – Adore the King; same as Amor Del Rey

ad seg - prison term for administrative segregation

agonies - withdrawal symptoms

ain't no thing - no problem, nothing to worry about; don't agree with you

AK - semi-automatic rifle, AK-47

AK47 - kill or murder

AKIA - KKK greeting, "A Klansman I am."

AKIGY - KKK greeting, "A Klansman Is Greeting You."

Alice - Aryan Brotherhood undercover name

Alice - LSD or mushrooms

Alice B. Toklas - marijuana brownie

All is Good/Well - motto of Vice Lords and People Nation

All is One - motto of Disciples and Folk Nation

all lit up - under influence of drugs

all star - user of multiple drugs

all that - possessing good qualities

always and forever - "Blood for Life"

amped and queer - high on coke or crystal meth

AN – Aryan Nation

ANP – American Nazi Party

answer up - respect your superiors and their orders

Anything going on? - Any drugs to sell?

AOK - always out killing

approved for the hood - approved for gang membership

ARM - Aryan Resistance Militia

asked for Nancy's hand - proposed for membership in
    Nuestra Familia
ate up - always wasted on drugs
A-town - Atlanta
Audi 5000 G - goodbye; peace out; Gangster - (see
    5000)
Aunt Hazel - heroin
Aunt Mary - marijuana
Aunt Nora - cocaine
avientate - "Just try it" or "Go for it."
ay yo trip - "Listen up; pay attention; check it out."

B
BEER - Bloods Eliminate Ericketts Roughly
B Queen - female associate of Bloods
B.I. - been incarcerated
babe-a-laba - close friend
baby bat - very young Goth
baby g or B.G. - baby gangster; very young gang
        member (usually under 12); new member who has
        not yet shot someone or proved himself
baby habit - occasional use of drugs
baby sit - guide someone through first drug experience
back the fuck up - stop, back off, watch out
bad bone - untrustworthy; don't trust him
bad go - bad reaction to drug
bag boy - sells dope for someone else
bag bride - crack-smoking prostitute
bag up - to package drugs in plastic bags; also hearty
    laughter
bagged up - arrested by police
balie - to fight
baller - high roller; one who sells a variety or large
    amounts of drugs
balling - vaginally implanted cocaine; having fun,
    getting high

bama - derogatory; country hick; poorly dressed;
    someone from Alabama
bandera -gang colors; bandana
bang/banging - gang activity; fighting, killing, stealing,
    selling drugs
banger - violent gang member
baptism - white supremacy term for initiation into gang
Barbara Jean -marijuana
barrio - (varrio) neighborhood
Bart Simpsons - LSD
base crazy - searching on hands and knees for loose
    pieces of crack
b-boy - non-gang member; one who dressing like gang
    member but only break dances
BDSM - Gothic term for Bondage, Discipline, Sado-
    Masochism
be down - agree; think the same way
be down for it - loyal to the gang; fight for the gang
be down with it- agreeing with; being a member of the
    gang
be geese - leave, as in, "We be geese"
be real - prepare for gang war, violence
beam me up, Scottie - crack dipped in PCP
beat artist - sells fake drugs
beat down - beating; usually gang initiation
bedbugs - fellow addicts
beef - crime; violation; problem; something that can be
    resolved by fighting
beggars - Blood term for Muslims
behind the scale - weigh and sell cocaine
beiging - altering of cocaine to appear higher purity
bend - prostitute
bender - drug party
bent - party, have fun, get drunk, high
berry - round red light on old police cars looked like a
    berry
BFL - Blood for Life

bibo - "Blood In, Blood Out" ("I'm BIBO")
big boy - important gang member
BIH - Burn in Hell; gang challenge
Billy Bad Ass - tough guy
birds - Bloods; hand signs imitating bird talons
biscuit - fifty rocks of crack
bit - time in jail
bitch - whore, woman, insult when directed to a male
bitch - conviction for being a habitual criminal, as in,
    "He got bitched."
bitch slap - shoot or beat enemy gang girl
bizzo - ugly girl; bizarre
blanks - poor quality drugs
blessed in - inducting person into gang who has
    rendered outstanding service to gang
bling bling - jewelry, from the sound it makes.
blobs - derogatory Crip nickname for Bloods
Blood - extremely violent gang; originated in Los
    Angeles
blood·clot - extremely bad; to die, be killed
blood in/ bloodied in - beating administered to recruit
    during Blood initiation; to slash or kill someone
blood out - to be beaten or killed as punishment for
    leaving Bloods
blow - cocaine or marijuana; to smoke cocaine or
    marijuana
blowman - gang member who does the shooting
Blue Birds - original name of Aryan Brotherhood gang
blue down - dressed down as Folk, Crip
blunt - fat joint; marijuana inside a cigar; marijuana and
    cocaine
body shop - correctional facility
body stuffer - one who ingests vials, balloons, or
    condoms filled with drugs escape detection
bogart a joint - salivate on a marijuana cigarette; refuse
    to share
bomb squad - crack-selling crew

bondage babe - Goth girl in fetish bondage clothes and
     gear
boo - marijuana
boo boo head - whore, deceitful woman
book - run, get away, leave
boost and shoot - steal to support a habit
boo-ya, boo-yah - totally great, incredibly fine; good
     crack
bopped up - high on angel dust
born Mecca - Five Percenter term for Baltimore
BOS - beat on sight; attack as soon as seen
BOS - Brothers of the Struggle
BOSS - Brothers of the Strong Struggle
bounce - leave hurriedly
boxed - in jail
bozak - penis, testicles
brace yourself - chill, fall back, stay cool
break - run, leave, escape
breakdown - shotgun; $40 crack rock broken and sold
     for $20
bro - affectionate term between Bloods
B-Town - Berkeley, California.
buck - shoot someone
bucket - old beat up car
bucky - shotgun
bumblebee - derogatory term for a Latin King
bummer trip - bad experience with drugs
bump - to tilt, as to tilt hat to show gang affiliation
bumper kit – girl's rear
bumping - looking good; refers to car with reverberating
     stereo
bumping titties - fighting
bunk - fake cocaine
burned - purchase fake drugs
burner - gang member known for shooting; also large,
     intricate grafitti
burning logs - smoking a joint

burnt - smoked too much weed
bust a cap - shoot at someone
bust this - listen to this; pay attention
busted - shot at someone; also arrested
buster - trying to be a gang member; fake gang
     member, weak person
bus ticket - gang hit, as to give him a bus ticket home
BWAP - bitch with a problem

C
CAT - Cripping All the Time
CFL - Crip for Life
C joint - where cocaine is sold
C Queen - female associate of Crip gang
C World - Crip World
C. O. - correctional officer
C.R.E.A.M. - acrynom; Cash Rules Everything Around
     Me; cream is money
C/S - con sofos; "Same to you", or "There's nothing you
     can do about it."
cacos - local thieves
carcel - jail
carnal(es) - brother(s)
chicano - Mexican American
chola - female gangster
cholo - slang for Mexican gangster
cuetes - gun, explosive, firecracker
Califas - slang for California
calo - Hispanic for Hispanic/English blended street
     slang
camarada - friend; homeboy, homegirl
candy - cocaine, crack, depressant, amphetamine
candy C - cocaine
candy flip - one hit of ecstasy added to three hits of
     LSD
candy land - correctional facility
cannon - huge marijuana joint

canoe - joint with hole in side or looks like a canoe
cap - shoot at; retort or answer
cap up - transfer bulk of drugs to capsules
car hop - girl who dates guy for his car
carcancha - old car, junker
carcel - penitentiary
canabis - marijuana
carnal - gang brother
carnala - female gang member
carnalismo - Hispanic term for gang brotherhood
carpet patrol - crack smokers searching the floor for
    crack
cartucho - package of marijuana cigarettes
cashed - empty bowl; drugs all consumed
Casper the ghost - crack
catch a cold - get killed
catch your back - keep watch behind you
cateye - a stud with women; one who stares sexually at
    a woman
cave boy - derogatory; early whites lived in caves
CeCe - Culver City Boys gang
CEG - .357 pistol
cell gangster - talks tough in jail, chicken when out
CFL - Crip for Life
chale - never mind, it does not matter
chalking - altering the color of cocaine to make it white
charged up - under influence of drugs
Charley - heroin
chaser - compulsive crack user
chaze - christen a new bowl or pipe
check - personal supply of drugs
check it out - listen to what I am saying.
checked in - initiated into a gang
cheese - money cheese
cheese out - snitch, give up
chicken scratch - searching on hands and knees for
    pieces of crack

chickenhead - dumb person who talks constantly
     (clucks) and wanders aimlessly; woman who
     performs oral sex
chill out - stop it; quit it; don't do/say/act like that.
Chill Town - Long Island
chilling - hanging out, relaxing, having fun, kickin' it
     chillun - smoking hashish or other drugs
China-eyed - eyes slanted from the influence of
     marijuana
catch a cold - get killed
chinga - la chinga, the damned activity; gang business
chingamos - f--k them up
chingasos - fighting, go to blows, a beating
chingate - f--k yourself
chip dog - gang member who skims money, drugs
chipper, chipping - occasional drug user
chipping - prison slang for having sex with a person
     other than regular sex partner
chivero - heroin addict
cho cha - vagina
chocolate - opium; amphetamine
chocolate city - Washington D.C.
chola - gang girl
cholo - modern pachuco gang member; Mexican
     gangster
chopper - assault weapon; AK-47
chota - police
chrome - hand gun
chrome - pistol
chrono - institutional write-up
chrono 115 - serious institutional write-up
chrono 128 - less serious institutional write-up
chubby - erection.
chucks - hunger after heroin withdrawal
chuco - pachuco; veterano, old time gang member
church - LSD paper imprinted with cross
cigarette paper - packet of heroin

circled - circled and beaten during gang initiation
CK - Crip Killer
claim - seek or claim gang membership
claim jumper - one who falsely claims gang
    membership
clear up - stop drug use
clica - gang, set
click in - gang initiation
click up - get along with other gang members
clocking dollars - making money by conducting gang
    business; selling drugs
clocking paper - making money selling drugs
closet baser - crack user who prefers anonymity
club - gang
cluck - cocaine smoker
cluck bucket - vehicle (often stolen) temporarily traded
    for drugs
coasting - under influence of drugs
cocktail - marijuana cigarette inside regular cigarette
cocoa puff - smoke cocaine and marijuana
cod - large amount of money
coke bar - bar where cocaine is openly used
cold storage - solitary confinement
cold shot - calculated, heartless action, committed with
    no concern or regard for others
colors – gang's colors, gang bandana
come correct - to do something the way it should be
    done
county blues - prison-issue clothes.
come home - come out of LSD trip
come with power - get ready to fight; bring weapons
coming out party - release from prison
coming out your face wrong - saying stupid things
commercial - Colombian marijuana
comps - homies, fellow gang members
con migo - someone I did time with

con sofos (C/S) - anything you say goes back to you
    twice as bad; so what?
connect - purchase drugs; supplier of illegal drugs
controzza - "The gang controls this area."
controzza con sotoas - gang neighborhood, territory,
    turf
coochie - vagina
cop - obtain drugs
cop shop - police station
copping zone - area where drugs are sold
coriander seeds - cash
corn stalker - marijuana in corn shucks, sealed with
    honey
cornflakes - cocaine
co-sign - approve
cotton - currency
course note - bill larger than $2
courted in - gang initiation
courted out - expulsion from gang by beating or death
cousin - fellow Crip (Cuzz)
cowboys - derogatory term for Texas Syndicate
crab - Blood derogatory term for Crips
crack - cocaine; from cracking sound when being
    "cooked"
crack attack - craving crack
crack gallery - place to buy crack
crack head - crack user
crack spot - place to purchase crack
crack star - crack user
crack queen - female crack addict who will perform sex
    and illegal acts to obtain money to buy drugs
cragared down - low rider vehicle
crank - mentally unstable person; also
methamphetamine
crap - Blood derogatory term for Crips
crap- low quality heroin
crash - sleep off effects of drugs

crazy - insane, or extremely daring, extremely violent
creeperbud - marijuana that creeps up on you
crew – gang
Crip - gang member
critter - the female role in a sexual prison relationship
crosshatch - code used to disguise messages
crossover - switch to another gang
crumbs - small pieces of rock cocaine
crumbsnatcher - junkie who steals tiny pieces of crack
crunch and munch - crack
cruzales - dissing term used by People for Folk gangs
C-Town - Cleveland, Ohio.
cuete - gun
cuz, cuzz - affectionate Crip term
curb service - selling drugs on street
custer/buster - false gang member
cut - dilute drugs
cut up - vagina
cuzzing - Cripping, being a Crip

D
D-Mecca - Five Percenter name for Detroit
da jungle - Brooklyn
da projects - prison, specifically Sing Sing
dabble - use drugs occasionally
daddy - marijuana joint
daddy mac - a cool guy, pimp daddy, da man, mac
    daddy
daisy roots - boots
damu - Swahili word for <u>blood</u>; adopted by Blood
    gangs, as in "I'm Damu."
dancing - fighting
dancing contest - fighting enemy gang
fighting with Emily - fighting with EME
dap - a high-five type of handshake; also power
de corazon - Neta gang term; "From the Heart"
dead presidents - currency

dead rag - Crip term for Blood colors

dedo - shoot middle finger at someone

deep - gang has many members

def, deft - gang term for death; looking good laid out; also feeling good; can make no mistakes

demonstration - gang fight

desert - Five Percenter term for New York

deuce - $2 worth of drugs

deuce & deuce, double deuce, deuce and a half - .25 caliber pistol

deuce and a quarter - Buick 225 vehicle

deuce two - .22 pistol

devil - enemy, usually referring to white people

devil bunny - Goth girl

devil's dick - crack pipe

dews - $10 worth of drugs

diablo - LSD paper imprinted with devil

diggidy - good herb

digie - scales used to weigh drugs

dillon - handgun

dime - 10 years in prison; also 1/16 ounce of marijuana; also means $10 bag of crack or marijuana

dime bag - $10 worth of drugs

dimed - informed to the police

dime dropper - snitch

ding him - sneak a swing at him

dipping - being nosey

dipping out - crack runners stealing a portion of drugs they carry

dirt grass - inferior quality marijuana

dirty bottle - positive urine test

dis, dissen, dissing - disrespect; not showing respect to gang member

dissed, dissed out - given no respect

Disciple Queen - female associate of Disciples

disease - drug of choice

diseased in - recruit required to have sex with persons
    with venereal disease or AIDS
dissed out - given no respect; to be disrespected
ditch weed - inferior quality marijuana, Mexican
    marijuana
divider - sharing a joint with someone
divorced - to get out of a gang
DK - Disciple Killer
do a buck 50 - speed out of a bad situation; go 150
    mph
do a ghost - leave the area quietly
do a joint - to smoke marijuana
do a line - to inhale cocaine
do a Rambo - violent attack on a person, usually using
    a weapon
do some work - do gang activity; rob; steal, fight
Double OG - second generation gangster
Do you want to ride? - verbal challenge to fight
DOC - definitely out of control
dog city - doing it for the money
dog pound - East Coast street gang
dog/dawg - Blood name for fellow gang member; good
    friend
doing a jack - committing a robbery
doing a pound - serving a five-year sentence
dollar - $100 worth of drugs
domestic - locally grown marijuana
don't fake claim – don't falsely claim gang membership
Dona Juana/Juanita - marijuana
do rag - nylon head scarf for hair grooming
dots - LSD or mescaline
doub - $20 rock of crack
double deuce - 22-caliber gun
double O.G. - second-generation gangster
doughnuts - People term for Black Gangster Disciples
down - connected with the gang; doing right by the
    homeboys; living up to gang expectations;

protecting gang turf; "It's a homeboy's job to be
down for the hood."
downed by Emily - killed by EME
down for mine - ability to protect self; willing to back
gang up in a fight
down for the hood - loyal to neighborhood/gang
down low - low profile
down with - in good standing with; agree with,
sympathetic
DPP - Disciples (or Dominicans) Don't Play
DQ - Disciple Queen
drag - ability to sweet talk girls
dragon - bad breath
drama - confrontation
draped - covered with gold jewelry (see "Turkish")
drive-on - verbally harass someone to get what one
wants
drinking forties - 40-ounce bottles of malt liquor
dripping - flaunting gang colors; dressed down
drop a dime - inform on someone; snitch
drop a lug on him - tell an inmate to act properly
drop the flag - quit the gang
drop some dew - provide urine sample for drug testing
drywall - fake drugs, or drugs so diluted that they are
worthless
D-town - Detroit
dub sack - $20 worth of marijuana
duck - woman
dugout - marijuana pipe
dukey rope - fat gold necklace, chain.
dummies - fake drugs
durag, do-rag - bandanna (gang colors) worn on head

E
E.Z. wides - extra wide rolling paper for marijuana
Easy go - easy job while in prison
eastly - very ugly

easy score - obtaining drugs easily
easy walkers - tennis shoes
eater - someone who eats marijuana
eeples - derisive Folks term to put down People gangs
efe - Spansh word for F; also refers to Nuestra Familia
eight - eighth letter of alphabet; heroin
eight (8)-track - 2 and ½ grams of cocaine
eight ball - 1/8 ounce of cocaine; also signifies drugs
    for sale
eight to the gate - paroled after 8 months of sentence
el estillo - "the style"; dressing in the gang style
el jale - the job
El Paso Tip - old Texas gang; currently refers to Texas
    Syndicate
el mas chignon - the f--kingest, toughest, macho male
Elaine - ecstasy
elbow - pound of marijuana.
eleven pointed pancake - Vice Lord who switched to
    Disciple
EME - phonetic for M; thirteenth letter of alphabet;
    Mexican Mafia
emeros - another name for Mexican Mafia
EMI - Mexikanemi prison gang
Emily - a Mexican Mafia member
ends - money
ENE - fourteenth letter of the alphabet; Northern
    Structure, Nortenos
ENE EFE - phonetic for the letters NF, meaning Nuestra
    Familia
ENE ERE - phonetic for the letters NR, meaning Norte
    Rules; Northern California Rules
enforzador - Latin King Enforcer; in charge of gang
    security
EPT - El Paso Tip gang
e-rickets - Blood term for Crips
Ese - "Hey" or "What's up?"
Ese's - Chicanos

ESE - Hispanic gang member; often used to refer to
     Texas Syndicate member
ESE TE - Sindicato Tejano (Texas Syndicate), or ST
Ese, Vato - Hey, Dude! Hey, Man!; refers to "that
     person"
ESE'S - slang name for Chicano gang members
esta mas loco - most crazy, the craziest
estar firme - go the ultimate for the gang; provide back-
     up in a fight or other bad situation
Este - ST, Texas Syndicate
estrella - a star tattoo, sometimes indicates that wearer
     has killed for the gang
Ever worked at McDonalds? - Ever been a member of
     Mexican Mafia?
everything is everything - everything is all right
EVL - executioner for Vice Lords
expect rain, thunder - expect serious trouble, extreme
     violence

F

factory - place where drugs are concocted, packaged,
     diluted
faded - disrespected
fag hag - homosexual woman who wants only
     homosexual friends
fair one - fair fight, evenly matched
faking claim - falsely claiming to be gang member
fall - arrested
false flagging - falsely claiming gang membership, or
faking enemy gang's sign to trick them
farmero - farmer; disrespectful term for Nuestra Familia
father time - prison court
fat pappy - fat joint or blunt
federated - Crip expression of disrespect for the color
     red
feed bag - marijuana container
fell down - got stabbed

feria/ferria - money, loose change
fifteen cents - $15 worth of drugs
finger wave - anal search by prison guards
fire it up - smoke marijuana
five-cent bag - $5 worth of drugs
five-dollar bag - $50 worth of drugs
five-plated - nickel plated handgun
f--ked up - high on drugs
flaco - nickname for skinny person
flag - gang bandana, gang colors
flagged in - recruit required to take rival gang's colors
    by violence
flake - cocaine
flashing - throwing gang signs
flashlight - police coming, police nearby
flat chunks - crack cut with benzocaine
flats - gold jewelry; links of gold chain
flip - betray, desert, turn against, quit on a friend or
    fellow gang member
flip the clip - put in work; shoot somebody
floating - driving fast
floods - disrespectful term for Bloods
flue - disrespectful term for blue
flue rag - blue/Crip bandanas/colors
fly - good looking
fly Mexican airlines - smoke marijuana
flying your colors/flying the flag - wearing gangs colors
FOI - fruit of Islam; Muslims
following that cloud - searching for drugs
foo - fool
foo-assed - stupid, dumb ass
foo foo stuff/dust - heroin; cocaine
foot soldier - ordinary gang member; lowest in the gang
four-five - .45 caliber pistol
four-twenty - 4:20 PM- marijuana; marijuana break
    time; National Marijuana Day (April 4th)
freak - pretty girl

freaking - wild sexual acts
free air - just released from prison
freeze - cocaine; renege on drug deal
fresh - good looking girl; PCP
Friday the Thirteenth - Attica Prison
frog - girl with no morals; jumps in any car; hops in any
    bed
front in - embarrass, put down another person
front off/up - in-your-face confrontation; face-to-face
    challenge
fronting on, with - pretending, putting up a false front
fry daddy - crack and marijuana; cigarette laced with
    crack
FTW - skinhead acronym for "Fuck The World"
fu - marijuana
FUBU - hip hop clothing company; acronym for "For U,
    By Us"; often with the number "05" for the five
    childhood friends who founded the company ; to
    Crips, stands for Folk Up Bloods Under
fugly - extremely ugly
full gear - flaunting gang colors; dressed down
full geat - geat is Blood term for gear

G
G - $1000 or 1 gram of drugs
G - gangster; what gang members call themselves;
    also, Five Percenters use "G" to represent God
gaffing - stealing; same as racking
gaffled - got cheated
g-down/up – gee'd up/down; dressed in gang colors
gaffle - to harass; to mess someone or something up
gag and frisky - whiskey
gage/gauge - marijuana; shotgun
game - criminal activity
gang bang - fight gang members; commit crime with
    other gang members, several have sex with one
gang banger - gang member

gangsta - gangster
gangsta lean - leaning down in car seat to hide as drive by
gasface - to show disrespect; make ugly face at someone
gated out - released from prison
gauge, gage - shotgun
gear - gang clothing
geek - person high on drugs
geeze - inhale cocaine
geezer - inject a drug
geezin a bit of dee gee - injecting drug
generic - fake
get a gage up - smoke marijuana
get a gift - obtain drugs
get burned - catch a sexually transmitted disease
get busy - have sex
get down - fight; inject a drug
get high - smoke marijuana
get in his face - butt in, intrude in somebody else's business
get in the groove - get things done
get jammed - accosted
get lifted - under influence of drugs
get off the gate - get it on; quit talking, start fighting
get paid - obtain money any way possible, robbery, burglary; gangs believe the world owes them something
get some digits - get telephone number
getting short - getting close to release date
get some gone - get out of my face
get spun - go partying
get stupid - act violently
get the wind - smoke marijuana
get through - obtain drugs
get your shine on - show your talent

get your swerve on - do something skillfully; to prepare
    to do something that you do well
getting some digits - obtaining telephone number
ghetto bird - police helicopter
ghetto sled - old, banged up car often covered with
    house paint.
ghetto star - drug dealer, gang celebrity
ghost - disappear, leave unobtrusively
ghost busting - searching for white particles in the
    belief is crack
ghost it - lose it
ghost town - Bronx
gift of the sun - cocaine
gig - gang gathering, party, dance, hanging out with
    gang
giggle smoke - marijuana
ginger snaps - Japanese
give wings - teach someone to inject heroin
glazed doughnuts - People/Brothers putdown of
    Gangster Disciples
gleeka - gang
g-male - female gang associate, member
g-man - Black Gangster
go AWOL - run away
going off - acting crazy
go in the sewer - inject drugs
go loco - smoke marijuana
go on a sleigh ride - inhale cocaine
go on green carpet - appear in court
go up on - fight; throw your hands up
gods - Five Percenter term for their male gang
    members (women affiliates are referred to as Earths)
go-fast - meth
going with Emily - leaving Nuestra Familia to join EME
going to visit Lugo - going to get killed
going 90 mph - peak of a drug trip
gone - ugly

good butt - marijuana cigarette
good giggles - marijuana
good go - proper amount of drugs for money paid
goofball - cocaine and heroin; depressant
goose - prison bus (i.e., Blue Goose, Gray Goose)
gopher - person paid to pick up drugs
got into town - arrived in prison
got it going on - successful gang member; successful
   gang event
government cheese - welfare
graduate - stop using drugs or progress to stronger
   drugs
graveyard - drug house out of drugs or shut down by
   police
grass/grass brownies - marijuana
grease - currency
green goods - paper currency
greens/green stuff - paper currency
g-ride - stolen car (grand theft auto)
grill - teeth
grip - gun
groceries - crack
growing daisies - dean
g-rock - one gram of rock cocaine
grogged - really stoned or burned out on marijuana
g-springs - gang car
g-star - ghetto star
g-ster - short for gangster
GTA - grand theft auto
Gucci - dressed in fine clothes
gump - homosexual
gun-up - get ready to fight
guns - muscular arms

H

H8 - hate (H+eight); as in "Don't Hate, Relate."
ham, hampster - Black person

ham sandwich - derogatory term for Muslims

hamburger - derisive term traditional Hispanic gang members call enemy Hispanic gang members who eat "white" food (Nuestra Familia call Mexican Mafia "hamburgers")

hamburger poisoning - killing Mexican Mafia gang member

hamster, ham - black person

hand-to-hand - direct delivery and payment

hard - unemotional; uncaring; tough, merciless

hard look - aggressive looks, challenging stare, maddogging

hardcore - extreme; big time, serious gangster

have a hard-on for - strongly dislike; as "The judge had a hard-on for him."

have heart - be fearless in dangerous situation

hawk - look hard at; stare down; challenging stare

hawk - nickname for Blood gang member

HBS - hanging, banging, slanging

He's from nowhere - has no gang affiliation; unprotected

head up - start a fight; fight someone

headhunter - female who does sexual acts for cocaine

Helen - heroin

heel and toe - go

henpecking - searching on hands and knees for crack

herb - marijuana; also a weakling, coward

herba - marijuana

hero - heroin

high numbers - large denominations of money

high rolling - making big money; dealing in drugs

highbeams - wide eyes of a person on crack

highside - to "dis" someone by ignoring him

hit - a killing

hit - crack; marijuana cigarette; to smoke marijuana

hit the main line/needle/pit - inject drug

hitter - small pipe designed for only one hit

hitting up - putting up graffiti; throwing gang signs
HO - half ounce of marijuana
holding - possessing drugs
holding aces - unarmed; needing a firearm
holding down - controlling turf, area
hold the unpaid bills - wait, do not kill him yet
homeboy/homie/homie, homes, honcho - friend, fellow
    gang member,
home grown - marijuana; also born in   the hood
honey - currency
honey blunts - marijuana cigars sealed with honey
honeymoon - early stages of drug use before addiction
hoo ride - drive-by shooting
hoochie - low-life woman
hood - neighborhood of gang member; gang, gang
    area
hoodies - gang members who wear clothes with hoods
hoodrat - sexually promiscuous girl; not respected
hooking vics - dissing, taunting Vice Lords
hook me up - set up a deal
hooked - addicted
hooked up - affiliated with gang
hooks - GD derogatory term for Vice Lords; also a
    phony, sissy
hoopty - car
hoo-rah - loud talking
hop a train - ride without paying
hopped up - under the influence of drugs
hot box - closed area filled with marijuana smoke
hot stepper - wanted by police; also pickpocket
house fee - money paid to enter crack house
house piece - crack given crack house owner as levy
how you sound - what did you say?
H-Town - Houston
hubba - rock cocaine
hubba pigeon - crack user crawling on floor searching
    for small pieces of dropped crack

huevos - Anglos
huff - inhalant
huffer - inhalant abuser (of gas, glue, paint)
hulling - using others to get drugs
hustle - attempt to obtain drug customers
hustler - individual out to make money or impress girls

I

ice cream habit - occasional drug use
illing – mental mistakes, acting weird, silly, stupid
in - connected with drug suppliers
in check - under control
in the clouds - high on drugs
in the hat - targeted to be killed
in the mix - involved in gang activity
Inca - highest ranking officer in Latin Kings
incense - opium
in pocket - carrying drugs for sale
insane - gang member who will kill
interplanetary mission - travel from one crack house to
    another in search of crack
issue - prison term for crime committed, such as,
    "What's your issue?"
issues - crack
IYAPNYAPN - acronym for gang motto, "If You Ain"t
    Pumpin' Nation You Ain't Pumping Nuttng"

J

jack - rob, steal, or assault; steal someone else's drugs
jacked up - beaten up, assaulted
jacking - robbery, assault
jackson - $20 bill
jailhouse punk - forced to become homosexual in
    prison
jailhouse turnout - heterosexual who becomes overtly
    homosexual or assumes female identity in prison
jakes - police

jalapeno - law enforcement officer in green uniform
jammed - confronted, accosted, detained
jamming - confrontational, coming on strong
jane - marijuana
JBAKE - John Brown Anti-Klan Committee; terrorist group
jefferson airplane - match split to hold partially smoked marijuana cigarette
jet - go, leave, run away
jiggable pie - female buttocks
jim jones - cocaine-laced joint dipped in PCP
jimmy - penis
jimmy hats - condoms
jitterbug - young gang fighter
jive - Black Gangsters' word for "five"
jive percenter - Five Percenter term for fake Five Percenter
jocker - aggressive, macho homosexual inmate who plays male role in homosexual relationship
jocking - following closely
johnny go fast - speed
joint - marijuana cigarette
joke signs - gang signs
jones - heroin
jonesing - need for drugs
joto - homosexual
JPT - on time, punctual; from Japanese People Time
Juan, Juanita - marijuana
juggle - sell drugs to support habit
juggler - teen-aged street dealer
juice - reputation, respect
juiced - car with hydraulics to raise and lower body
jump street - from the beginning
jumped in - initiation into a gang
jungle - prison recreation yard
jura (juda) - police

K

K-9 - correctional officer
kabuki - crack pipe made from a plastic bottle and
    rubber sparkplug cover
Kansas - Kill All Nigga Suck Ass Slobs
keep it moving - forever represent your set
key - kilo of cocaine
keister stash - drugs, weapons, other contraband
    hidden in the anus, usually inside a rubber balloon
keyed - high on drugs
kibbles & bits - crumbs of crack
kick - stop using drugs
kicks - shoes
kick you down - give you something, set you up in drug
trade
kicked - passed out or about to pass out
kicking it - relaxing, partying with fellow gang members
kicks - tennis shoes
kiddie dope - prescription drugs
kindergoth - very young Goth member, or one posing
    as a Goth member; a wannebe Goth
kindred - white supremacy term for fellow member of
    gang
kit - equipment to inject drugs
kite - illegal written correspondence; secret gang
    information
kluckhead - crack addict
knocking bitches - having sex
knots - money, usually $100's
knuckle samich - fat joint of marijuana
knuckle up - get ready to fight
kool - everything all right
KOS - kill on sight

L

lady from Bristol - pistol
L.A. sag - wearing pants extremely low

la ley - police
la llanta - Black person, fat person; like a tire
la mas chingona - the toughest (female) or the top dog
land of no return - dead
la ruca, la loca - female gang member; crazy female
laces - chrome, spoke rims
lady - girlfriend
lambiche - one who sucks up, a kiss ass
lamborghini - crack pipe made from plastic rum bottle
    and a rubber sparkplug cover
LC - Latin Counts; enemy gangs call them Latin
    Cowards
lamping - hanging out by street lamp
lapped - sitting in laps in crowded vehicle
large - important; recognized; famous; rich; respected
lay pipe - have sex
layout - equipment for taking drugs
leaning - showing effects of drugs
leaping - under influence of drugs
learn and look - a book
learys - LSD
legal speed - over the counter asthma drug
legal yard - area where permission has been received
    to post grafitti
let's bail - let's leave
let's ride on someone - seek any enemy gang member
    for retaliation
LHOSR - People Nation acronym for Love, Honor,
    Obedience, Sacrifice, Righteousness
lice - Blood derogatory term for Crips
lid - one ounce of marijuana
lifeboat - pardon
life on the installment plan - life sentence in prison
Lincoln - $5 bill
lined - initiation requiring recruit to run gang gauntlet
live hook up - phone call to/from prison
lizard butt - ugly girl

LLLWUK - Folk Nation motto; "life, liberty loyalty,
    wisdom, understanding, knowledge"
loc - loco, crazy muthafuka
loc'ed; loc'ed out - acting crazy, loco
loc'ing in - "locking in"; Crip word for commiting crime in
    front of gang as initiation
locker knocker - inmate who steals from other inmates
loco - crazy; gang member who will do almost anything
locs - sunglasses
locoweed - marijuana
Locs/loks - dark sunglasses worn by locos, crazies who
    will do anything (Crips - Locs; Bloods - Loks)
lollypops - putdown word used to dis other gangs
looking - looking for violence, drugs, opportunities
lop - prison term for newcomer
Lord Allah - Five Percenter name for Los Angeles
los pinchis placas - the fucking pigs, police
Love, Mom - Vice Lords acronym; Love, Obedience,
    Victory, Equality, Money, Overcome, (struggle of)
    Minorities
low budget - cheap date; poor quality drugs
low rider - unimportant hanger-on involved in gang
    activity
LQ - Latin Queen
lucky charms - ecstasy
Lugo's pad is up to (a number) - enemy gang has killed
    (a number) of Nuestra Familia gang members
lunchbox - kids that do drugs
lynch mob - a gang

M

M - Mexican Mafia; marijuana; morphine
M&M - depressant
Mac 10 - submachine gun pistol
mac daddy - cool guy
mac/mack - ability to sweet talk girls
mack - weapon

mad dog/maddogging - glaring challenges to intimidate
     enemy gang; dissing, hard looks; crossing out other
     gang's graffiti
made his bones - killed upon gang's order for
     admission into gang
mad scientist - someone who makes crank
main man - best friend, backup
make it hot - prepare for gang fight, gang war, drive-by
     shooting
make up - need to find more drugs
making bank - making money; illegal activity
mama - female motorcycle gang groupie who provides
     sex to all members (also called a sheep)
Man, The Man - police
man with a grudge - a judge
marano - Hispanic word meaning pig, referring to law
     officers
mari - marijuana cigarette
maricon - Hispanic word for homosexual
marimba - marijuana
mark - wannabee gang member; one who will cross
     over to another gang; disloyal person
married - join a gang
Mary, Mary Jane, Mary Jonas - marijuana
Mary Mitchell - Mexican Mafia
mash it up - you handle it
matchbox - marijuana
Master, The - Latin King term for crowned head tattoo
maxing and relaxing - being cool; being calm,
     deliberate
Mecca - gang name for Harlem, NY
Medina - Five Percenter name for Brooklyn, NY
Meg/Megg/Meggie - marijuana
mega flex - erection
Member of Mecca - tattoo worn by some 5 Percenters
merchandise - drugs
mesa - the youthful offender board

mess 'em up - beat someone up

Mexican saddle pards - Mexican Mafia

mi vida loca - "My Crazy Life"; acceptance of gang
    ideology and way of life; live for now and don't
    worry about the consequences; is symbolized by
    three dots, usually on web of hand between thumb
    and finger

Miss Emma - morphine

mission - going into enemy territory; drive-by shooting;
    trip out of crack house to obtain crack

mix - what is happening, as "in the mix"

MJ - marijuana (Mary Jane)

MM - Mexican Mafia; also, Mariano Maravilla, a
    neighborhood gang in Los Angeles

MMM - Money, Macks (weapons); Murder; or Money
    Mayhem, Murder; or Making More Money

MMMSMB - more money, more sex, more bitches

moan and groan - telephone

Mo - Moorish; member of El Rukn gang; El Rukn gang
    greeting, as in, "What's up, Mo?"

Mo's - mojados; undocumented Mexican Nationals

MOB - Member of Blood

mobbing - Blood word for doing Blood business

mobile - proper, nice looking

mojado - illegal immigrant

moniker - street name, gang name, nickname

monkey - drug dependency; messed up on drugs

monos - cigarette made from cocaine paste and
    tobacco

mop and pail - jail

morning wake-up - first blast of crack from pipe

Morocco - Five Percenter name for Seattle

mosco - fly, mosquito; also derisive Nuestra Familia
    term for Mexican Mafia members

Mother of God - LSD paper with naked woman imprint

move on - challenge or physical attack; to mess with
    someone

movie star drug - cocaine
MSB - money, sex, bitches
mucho pedo - big ruckus, much trouble
mud duck - very ugly girl
muerte - overdose of drugs
mule - carrier of drugs, weapons
munchies - become very hungry after smoking drugs
mushroom - innocent bystander shot in drive-by
    shooting
mutt - male slut
my bad - my fault; my mistake
my man - my friend
my nine - 9mm semi-automatic pistol

N
N/A - new arrival
N/H - neighborhood
nailed - arrested
Nancy Flores - NF, member of Nuestra Familia
nation - regional or national gang confederation
nel - no
Nelson Franklin - Nuestra Familia
nester - Nuestra Familia gang member
new jack - new gang member; has not made his bones
    yet
New Jerusalem - Five Percenter name for New Jersey
nick/nickel - 0.5 grams of marijuana
nickel - five-year prison sentence
nickel bag - $5 worth of drugs; heroin
nickel bags - derogatory term for Five Percenters
nickel note - $5 bill
nigga - "*Never Ignorant Getting Goals Accomplished*"
nina/neenah - 9 mm pistol
nine mike/9 mike - 9 mm pistol
no chinges – Don't mess/f--- with me
no diggity - no doubt, without question, correct, for sure
no esta limpio - not clean; not drug-free

no grato - not wanted
nod - effects of heroin; as "on the nod"
NOI - Nation of Islam; Black Muslims
Norte 14 - Northern California Hispanic gang
Norteno - same as Norte 14
nose candy - cocaine
nose drops - drugs, narcotics, liquefied heroin
nose powder/stuff - cocaine
nothing but gangster - pure, real, all-out gangster
nothing but niggar - 100% Blood gang member
nucker - dumb person
number 9 - ecstasy
nut up - angry; mad at someone

O

O - opium; ounce of any drug
OB - Original Banga; original gangster, old time
    gangster
obo-ing - drinking robotussin with codeine (also termed
    robo-ing)
off brands - enemy gang set
OG - Original gangster; same as OB
okie dokie - to rob, cheat, or con
Old Bird - mother
Old Jude - father
Old Lady - wife, girlfriend of motorcycle gang member
ones and twos - shoes
on hit/swoll - good, slamming, excellent
on ice - in jail
on my dick/jock - follow closely, copy poorly
on the bricks - out of prison
on the nod - stoned on narcotics
on the outs - out of prison, detention
on the pipe - free-basing cocaine
on the real - honest, truthful
on the sneak tip - to watch secretly
on the strength - based on the facts

one box tissue - one ounce of crack
one time - police officer; tells you only one time; one
    chance to get out alive
oo-lahs - Crip term for Bloods
OOZE - Uzi weapon
Open the line - start communicating
Ophelia Pratt - female rat, snitch
OPP - other people's property
Opposites - enemies
Orgullo Mexicano - Mexican Pride; used by Border
    Brothers
other apartments - other prisons
other side of the line - enemy gang
O-Town - Orlando
out of pocket - caught unaware
OZ - Outlaws gang; drugs by the ounce, or person
    selling drugs; symbol that drugs can be bought at
    this place

P

P's - Pachucho gang members
p - peyote, PCP
P.C. - protective custody
P.O. - parole officer
P/P's - Pachucos
paca - rat pack; gang assault
pachucos - Hispanic gang members; also El Chuco (El
Paso)
packing - carrying firearm, drugs
pack your s--t - get ready to move; gather belongings
pal - parolee at large
panic - drugs not available; users frantic
paper blunts - marijuana in paper casing
paperboy - heroin peddler
paps - rolling papers
participate - help gang member in fight
party lights - police car lights

payback - retaliation, vendetta, revenge
Pe Ce - PC (protective custody)
peace in - not looking for trouble
peace out - goodbye, see you later
peanut butter - PCP mixed with peanut butter
peckerwood - putdown word for white person; cracker
peddler - drug supplier
pedo – fight
peeps – people; my associates
pee wee - crack; $5 worth of crack
peel - kill someone; to get peeled
peeling caps - shots to the head often peel the cranium
    away
peep - PCP; also look at, listen up; also Five Percenter
    term for new recruit
peeps - people; friends, associates
peewees - young gangsters; baby gangsters; young
    gang affiliates or members used as runners,
    lookouts, or couriers of weapons and drugs
pelon - a hard pull; also bald, baldy
pendejo - fool, imbecile
People - large gang nation, originated in Chicago
Pepsi habit - occasional use of drugs
permafried - high all the time
perpetrate - betray, shame yourself or the gang
perros - dogs; slang for cops
pescados - fish; Hispanic gang word for new members
phat - incredible, great, fine, wonderful
pianoing - using fingers to feel around for find lost crack
PID- possession with intent to distribute
piece - one ounce; cocaine; crack; firearm
pig pen - code to disguise messages
pink look - young inmate; also called a cherry
pimp daddy - cool guy, well dressed
pimp your pipe - lend or rent your crack pipe
pimped out - well-dressed person
pinacates - Black people

pinga - prick
pinta - Hispanic gang term for jail, prison
pipe - penis
Piru - L.A. Blood gang; Crips call them "pussies in red
     uniforms"
piss and punk - bread and water diet
pizza toppings - psychedelic mushrooms
PJ's - projects; low rent housing
PK - Piru Killer
placas - graffiti or gang name in graffiti
planning marriage - Aryan Brothers prepping recruit
play yourself - reveal a weakness; playing your cards
     too soon;
player - individual out to make money, impress girls;
     someone in the mix
plo - present location
plow the deep - get some sleep
pocket rocket - marijuana
POD - past overdose; dead
poo butt - sissy
poof - smoking ice
poor box - prison slang for box holding items taken
     from other inmates
poor man's pot - inhalant
pop goes the weasel - kill someone
popped - arrested
pop off - one who commits random acts of violence
popo - police
popped a cap - shot at someone
popping collars - showing off to impress others
ports - windows of automobiles; as gun ports
por vida (P/V) - gang member for life; Spanish
     translation: "For Life, Forever"
posse - East Coast term for a gang, crew
potato butt - girl with big hips
pothead - someone who smokes marijuana
pregnant - a fat joint with a lump in the middle

prescription - marijuana cigarette
primo - marijuana joint laced with cocaine; also number
     one
progeny - white supremacy term for probationary
member
program - prison term for how a prisoner does his time
project gold - huge gold hoop earrings
props - proper respect
pruno - alcoholic drink made by prisoners
psycho - a gang member who enjoys killing
P-Town - Patterson
puff/puff the dragon - smoke marijuana
pugging - fighting
pull a train - gang initiation of female; has sex with all in
     gang
pull a will - vomiting from too much drug use
pullers - crack users who pull at parts of their bodies
pulling you on - making a fool of you
pumping - selling crack
punk/punkin - pervert, weakling, coward
pure - heroin
puro 13 – pure south California gang member
 push - sell drugs
push shorts - cheat on drug sale; provide less drugs,
     sell short
pusher - one who sells drugs; metal hanger or umbrella
     rod used to scrape residue in crack stems
put in check - discipline someone
put in work - gang activity, mission; generally a
     shooting
put that on the set - prove what you are saying is true
put your s--t on the street - tell your secrets to everyone
puta - prostitute
puto - homosexual
puto mark - crossing out (disrespecting) enemy gang's
     graffiti

PV - Spanish for "Por Vida"; in the gang for life, for
   always

Q
Q.P. - quarter pound of marijuana
quail or queen - passive homosexual
quarter bag, piece - 1/4 ounce or $25 worth of drugs
quarter-o - quarter ounce of marijuana
Que hubole? – What's happening?
Que la chingada? - What the f—k!
Que la fregada - What the hell is this mess?
Que relaje - a major embarrassment; also a snitch
Que se vaya – Just get out of here
queen - female gang member
Queen Bee - Blood term for Latin Kings
queeted - getting too high off half a bowl
quemar - to snitch; to "burn" someone by telling on
   them
quette - gun
quiet it's kept - known, talked about only clandestinely
quick discharge - killed
quoted - number of minutes recruit is beaten during
   gang initiation

R
rack, rack up - shoplift in large quantities
rag - gang colors, usually bandana
ragged - wearing gang colors, usually bandana
railroad station - court
AHOWA - Racial Holy War; symbol of white
   supremacists
rain and thunder - gang violence
rain check - parole
rainy day woman - marijuana
raise - leave
Rambo gauge - sawed-off shotgun
rap - criminal charge; to talk with someone

raspberry - female who trades sex for crack
rat - someone who turns drug dealers in to the police
rat hunter - person assigned to hunt down, punish
    snitches
rat packing - many attacking few
rata - Hispanic term for a female informant; a snitch; rat
rave - party designed to enhance drug scene; popular
    party craze
razed - under the influence of drugs
real nigga - true gangster
recompress - change cocaine flakes to resemble "rock"
recruit - look for good-looking girls
red eye - glare at someone, challenge
red phosphorus - speed prepared to smoke
Red Rider - Blood term for female gang member
red rum - murder, spelled backwards
red zone - get ready to fight; prepare for war; war zone
relatives - Blood term for homeboys
rents - parents
repping - representing, as in, "Repping LK"; (I'm a Latin
    King.)
rescue Hoover - gang initiation; recruit must retrieve six
    pennies while fighting six gang members
respect - fear; what gang members want from other
    people
Reyes - Kings; street name for Latin Kings
rice and beans - Puerto Ricans
ride - vehicle
ride on, rode on - drive to enemy neighborhood for
    drive-by shooting
rifa, rifamos, rifan - "We rule/reign", "We are the best"
riffing on - making fun of, joking, kidding
rig - equipment used to inject drugs
right hand soldier - Black Gangster Disciple lieutenant
righteous - correct, true
righteous bush - marijuana

RIP - sign of past or impending violence; sometimes a
    roll call (listing) of names of gang members who
    have been killed or a list of the enemy targeted for
    killing
rip off - steal, take; often refers to ripping off drugs
ripped - under the influence of drugs
ripped off - prison term for forcible anal sex
rivithead - Goth who loves certain type of Gothic music
roach clip - clip for partially smoked marijuana cigarette
roach - marijuana butt
road dog - close friend, homie, partner
robo-ing - drinking robotussin with codeine
rock - crystallized cocaine
rock attack - craving for crack
rock house - place where crack is sold and smoked
rock star - cocaine prostitute; female who trades sex for
    crack or money to buy crack
rockafella - rock him to sleep; kill him
rocket - marijuana cigarette
Rockette - female who uses crack
Rodney King - to deliberately provoke police brutality
roid rage - aggressive behavior caused by excessive
    steroid use
roll - hang with, associate with
roll 'em up/rolled up - arrested/ forced out of an area
rollers - police
rolling - doing well; having a nice car
rolling deep - many gang members in vehicle
Rolling O's - the Rolling 10's through Rolling 90's
    gangs
rolling one time - police are coming
rook - person who can't hang (can't handle) his/her
    drugs
rooster - crack; also Piru Blood gang member
rope - marijuana

RTD - ghetto busses (Rapid Transit District); like
    busses, gang members are rough, tough, and
    dangerous
ru, roo - Rooster; Piru Blood gang member
Ruby Red - girl, woman, bitch
ruka - gang chick
runners - people who sell drugs for others
rush - ability to sweet talk girls, put moves on girls

S
S.O.S. - shoot on sight
S'up? – What's up/What's going on?
SA - stands for "ESE"; or "essay"; slang for Hispanic
    gang member
sack chaser - woman using a man for his money
Sackett - AB gang member
sagging - wearing pants very low; gangstering
sagging LA style - wearing pants extremely low
salami - derogatory term for Muslims
salto - a jump in gang initiation
salty, you - you think you know everything
Sam - federal narcotics agent
Sammy Davis, Jr. - boot licking
sasafras - marijuana
satch - saturated with drug solution to smuggle drugs
    into prisons or hospitals
Satin Disciple - white Disciple gang member
scandalous - deadbeat; bad person
scank - terrible person, awful person
scary dudes - Latin Kings
Scooby Doo - a marijuana blunt
scraps - derogrotory term Norte uses to put down Sur
gang members
sends his regards - individual has been caught,
    imprisoned, or killed and can no longer be counted
    on for assistance

set tripping - betraying or killing a member of your own
    gang, but who is a member of a different set, as
    from another community
shank - prison word for knife
shaolin - gang term for Staten Island
sherm - PCP, crack; cigarette dipped in embalming
    fluid
shit - marijuana, drugs in general
shoot/shoot up - inject drugs
shooter - person who uses a gun
shooting gallery - place where drugs are used
shooty - shotgun
Shorty Boys, shorty, shorties - members of a certain
gang; also young people who sell drugs on the streets;
also girls
shot down - under influence of drugs
shotcaller - person in charge, older, proven, successful
    gang member
shotgunning - putting joint in mouth backwards and
    blowing the smoke into another person's mouth.
shotty - shotgun.
Shout/shout out - greeting, acknowledgement
shovel time - time to kill or bury someone
Show and prove - demonstrate, prove, show us
Shu - prison term for security housing unit
Siamese - two-faced person
Simon - yes
Six pack - police lineup of six people
six-o-two - 602; prison term for inmate appeal form
skanless - low life behavior; cowardly skirmish or attack
skeeger/skeezer - crack-smoking prostitute; ugly girl
sketch - bad reaction to LSD or marijuana
sketching - very nervous; returning from speed-induced
    high
skied - under the influence of drugs
skies - scales used to weigh drugs
skin popping - injecting drugs under the skin

slack - bag of drugs that don't weigh out
slam - inject a drug
slamming - dynamic, outstanding, excellent
slanging - selling drugs on the streets
sleeved - arms covered with tattoos
sling/slang - deal or sell drugs
slipping - not being alert, not paying attention
slobs/slops - terms used by Folks and Crips to dis
    Bloods
slow your roll - relax, take it easy, don't be so upset
SMM - sex, money, murder
SMMM - sex, money, more money, murder
smoke - kill someone
smoke you out - smoke marijuana with you
smoked him - shot him, killed him
smoker - person who smokes cocaine
smurfs - white people
snaps - money
snite - lighter used to smoke drugs
snizzle - snitch
snoop - Crip name for Blood
snort - to inhale cocaine; use inhalants
snot - residue produced from smoking amphetamine
snot balls - rubber cement rolled into balls, burned, and
    sniffed for high
sow - cocaine; heroin; amphetamine
snow bunny - white female
snow cone - ice pick to be used as a weapon
social - social worker
society high - cocaine
soflon - informant, stitch, stool pigeon
softballs - depressant
soldier - lowest member of gang; does as ordered
solidas - female associates of Los Solidos gang
soma - PCP
sopers - depressant

souljas - Black Disciples Gang Nation members
    (soldiers)
space cadet - someone high on drugs
spaced out - high on marijuana
speed - methamphetamine; crack
speed freak - habitual user of meth
spice - Crip term used to refer to themselves
spoc - police officers (cops spelled backwards)
sporting - to inhale cocaine
spray - inhalant
springs - vehicle
ssay - slang for ESE, a Hispanic gang member
stab out - leave.
stackola - money; stacks of money
stall it out - stop what you are doing
stash - place to hide drugs, guns, stolen goods
steerer - person who directs customers to crack seller
step off - back away from a confrontation
step to - get into a fight
step up - walk into a confrontation
stinkweed/stinky - marijuana
stoned - under the influence of drugs
stoner - someone who stays high on marijuana
str8 - (str+eight) real, serious, straight
straight up - telling the truth
strapped - carrying a firearm
strawberry - cocaine prostitute; trades sex for crack
stroll - out on parole
stuffing - hiding drugs anywhere you can
styling and profiling - well-dressed and showing off
sucker - one who is afraid to fight
Sudan - Five Percenter name for Dallas
suffering needing bufferin - having problems
Sur - south, or southside, or Sureno gang
Sur 13 - Hispanic gang from Southern California
Sureno - same as Sur 13 above
surat - derogatory term for Surenos

SWASS - acronym; "Some wild-ass silly shit"; crazy
    scheme, far out behavior
sway-boy - Crip name for Blood
swisher - hollow cigar filled with marijuana.

T
T4L - thug for life
tabs - LSD
Taco Bell – "Take All Crips Out - Bloods Usually Live
    Longer"
tacs - tattoos
tag - gang member's secret or street name; to graffiti
tagger - a person who writes graffiti
tagging - writing graffiti
tail - prison term for parole or parole officer
take him to the box - kill him
take no shorts - let no one take advantage of you
take to the box - kill someone; put someone in a coffin
talking from the heart - honest and serious,
    accompanied by hitting chest while throwing gang
    signs
talking head - argue, wanting to fight
talking smak/smack - aggressive words
talking trash - saying angry, rude things
tar - opium; heroin
tats, tacs - tattoos
tax - rob, steal
taxing - price paid to enter a crack house; charging
    more for drugs depending on race/economics of
    customer or if not a regular customer
tea - marijuana, PCP
tea party - to smoke marijuana
teardrops - crack packaged in cut-off corners of plastic
    bags
tecato - Hispanic word for heroin addict
tech - nine mm gun
tech nine - nine mm gun

teenager - 1/16 ounce of cocaine
term - prison word for sentence or for credit for work
Terror Dome - Attica Prison
Texas pot, tea - marijuana
TG - tiny gangster; young or new gang member
THC - The Hispanic Connection gang; also marijuana
Theresa Sanchez - TS (Texas Syndicate) member
 thick like quick - Blood saying: come quickly
Third Coast - Gulf Coast area
Thirteen - marijuana; 13th letter of alphabet; M for EME
Thoroughbred - drug dealer who sells pure narcotics
Three G - third generation gangster
Throw down - insult enemy by throwing their signs
     upside down
throw up - throw own gang sign up; grafitti an area
     quickly
thug life - gang life; popular gang tattoo
thugs - inmates who challenge guards; also criminal
     gang members
thumper - gun
thumpers - hand made brass knuckles
ticket to Lugo's pad - slated for death
tight - good
tin - container for marijuana; tinfoil marijuana pipe
tipped up - gang affiliated; to associate with or join a
     gang
tiptoe through your tulips - transferring to your prison
to the curb - bad situation; no money; no drugs
toke/toke up - inhale cocaine; smoke marijuana
tonto - Hispanic for dummy, idiot
tools - equipment used for injecting drugs
topped out - off parole
torch is lit - gang hit going down
torch up - smoke marijuana
torcido - arrested, busted, jailed, imprisoned
TOS - Terminate on Sight; death warrant
toss up - girl used for sex; trades sex for crack

tout - person who introduces drug buyers to sellers
track thirteen - life sentence
track/tracks - row of scars or scabs from drug needles
trank - PCP
trap - hiding place for drugs
trashed - under the influence
trashed some trees - smoked marijuana
travel agent - LSD supplier
Trecé - Spanish for "13"; Southern California gang
trees - marijuana or pot
trey eight/Tray eight - .38 caliber gun
trick - phony, sissy, prostitute
tried - challenged by someone
trip - drug-induced condition; too much; something else
triple o - Blood gang member
Triple O.G. - third generation gangster
true that - truthful statement
TTTT - Asian gang motto; tihn (love), tien (money), tu
     (prison), and toi (crime)
turf - neighborhood, gang area, place where drugs are
     sold
Turkish - wearing heavy, ornamental gold jewelry, also
     called "flats"
turned on - introduced to drugs; under the influence
turned out - sexually assaulted by another inmate
turning out - disrupting with violence
Tutti-Frutti - flavored cocaine
tweak mission - on a mission to find crack
tweaker - crack user looking for rocks on the floor
tweaking - out of drugs; drug-induced paranoia;
     peaking
twenty/twenty cents - $20 rock of crack
twenty-four and seven - prison term for all day, all week
twist - marijuana cigarette
twist and twirl - girl
two for nine - two $5 vials or bags of crack for $9
Two G - Second generation gangster

U
UBL - Undying Blood Love
UC ride - plain gang car
Ugs - Crip term for Bloods
Ultimate - crack
Una chavalona - young, good-looking female
uncle - federal agent
underdogs - prison inmates
undergrad - convict, inmate
unit - one bag of dope
up against the stem - addicted to marijuana
up from the shoulder - fight with fists
up on it - to know about something; particularly in the
     know about drugs; successful in dealing drugs
uppers - amphetamine
Uz - Uzi weapon

V
V - valium
Valentine - short prison sentence
V/L - vida loca, gang member for life; also initials of
     Vice Lords
vamp - leave
varrio - Spanish word for neighborhood; corruption of
     barrio
vato - Hispanic word for man, boy, guy, dude
vato loco - Hispanic term for crazy person, crazy dude,
     crazy gangster, will do anything, one who is with it
vendidos - Hispanic for traitor, snitch, one who has sold
     out
vest - condom
veterano - veteran gang member
vic - victim
vida loca - crazy life; gang life; gang member for life
Vikki Lou - derogatory term for a Vice Lord

violation/violated - breaking gang rules, punishment for
    breaking rules; failure to dis enemy gang member
visit Lugo - killed

W
wacky tobacky - marijuana
wadded up - stoned, high on drugs
wak - incorrect or substandard graffiti
walkie - male role in homosexual relationship
walking the line - gang initiation; jumped in, beaten
    down
walls - prison
wannabe - apprentice gang member, a pretender; one
    trying to impress others as gang member
war wagon - vehicle carrying gang weapons
WASH - White American Skinheads
wasted - stoned out on drugs
watchalo - watch it; watch out
wuz up – what's up? What's happening?
weak - not good
wearing the brand - sporting gang tattoo
weed out - weed for sale
weekend Goth - one who dresses normally around
    others and as a Goth only when attending Goth
    functions
went out - did something stupid, unacceptable
West Asia - Five Percenter name for San Francisco
wet - bleeding
wet 'em up - make someone bleed; stab or shoot them
wet cha - caused you to bleed
whadup, Dawg - Blood gang greeting
what it "B"? what it "B" like? - Blood greeting; uses no
    "C"s
what it "C?" what it "C" like? - Crip greeting; uses no
    "B"s
what it "G"? - Gangster greeting
Where you from? - to what gang do you belong

Who brought you home? - Who jumped you into the
    gang?
wigger - derogatory term for people who try to act black
What up? What's up?- What's happening?"
wiggin - needing drugs
wilding - one who lives on the street, gets into trouble
wildstyle - complicated interlocking graffiti
witsec - witness security program
wolf - aggressive homosexual
Womb to Tomb - Blood 4 Life; Blood forever
word - absolutely, true, OK
word to the mother - earnest promise of truthfulness
word up - emphasizes that something is not a lie
worked in Frisco - did prison time in San Quentin
working - conducting gang business; committing
    criminal acts
works - equipment for injecting drugs
WOTAN - Will Of The Aryan Nation; white supremacist
    symbol
Writer - graffiti artist

X

X - marijuana; MDMA; amphetamine

Y

Yellow submarine - marijuana
Yerba - marijuana
YG - young gun; new gang member
YGB - Young Gifted Brother
yokes shrunk - gang is losing members and power
yo que, puto - "So what, queer?"
Yo! - Hey!/Listen up!/Yes!/OK
you played yourself - did yourself wrong
yoked - muscular, built up from body building
yuppie flu - ongoing effects of snorting cocaine

Z

z - 1 ounce of heroin
z - frequently replaces the letter "s" in
    graffiti, speech
zacate - marijuana (grass)
zig zag - move out; leave quickly
zip - one ounce of any type drug
ZOG - Zionist Occupational Government
zoinked - intoxicated on drugs to the point of
    uselessness
zombie - PCP; heavy user of drugs
zoom - PCP; marijuana laced with PCP
zoomers - individuals who sells fake crack and then
    runs away
Zulu - Zulu Nation; Black Americans

15. The Future of Gangs

Recent Trends

- Younger and younger active members (eight or nine years old)
- Ethnic and racial crossover in multiethnic neighborhoods
- Insurgence of female gangs
- Growth of gangs in suburban communities
- Acquisitions of larges sums of money from illegal activities
- Increased use of drugs and alcohol
- Use of more organized guerrilla warfare tactics and more powerful weapons
- Increasingly total disregard for human life; lack of remorse; consequences do not matter

Future Trends

1. Local gangs will continue to evolve from criminal street gangs to organized crime status.

2. All time highs will be reached in gang violence and drug activity.

3. Violence will be carried out with more sophisticated communication, weapons, and procedures.

4. Gangs will utilize the newest and best technology in their activities.

5. Big time gangs will become more business oriented and use more legitimate businesses as fronts for gang activity.

6. Gang membership will increase, particularly during recessions and depressions.

7. Youth will become gang members at younger and younger ages.

8. More members remain active in their gangs longer than before, well past their twenties and into their forties.

9. Gangs will change their traditional characteristics and identification methods in order to better escape detection; new me\methods will arise.

10. The number and type of racially motivated gangs and hate groups will increase, and they will find new groups to hate and mistreat.

11. There will be marked increases in the number of female gangs and the number of female gang members in both all-female and co-ed gangs.

12. Gang members will outnumber and out-gun available law enforcement authorities.

13. Street gangs and prison gangs will become more closely aligned and subsequently more powerful both inside prisons and in the public.

14. Courts and prisons will be overloaded with gang cases; probation and parole officers will be swamped with gang cases.

15. Female gangs will become more common, more independent of male gangs, and more involved in more serious crimes.

16. Gang growth and violence will increase as the drug trade increases.

17. Youth gangs will become more organized and a greater threat to society.

18. Gang members will enter the gangs at earlier ages and remain active in gangs longer, with gangs eventually having a higher percentage of adult members.

19. Gangs will become more sophisticated and organized, and will attempt to cover their criminal activities behind the guise of community service or legitimate business corporations.

20. Gangs will be less ethnically pure.

21. Adult prison gang members returning to their communities will create, recreate, or energize local youth into more organized and dangerous gangs.

22. Few communities will have programs that will deal effectively with gangs.

23. Gangs and gang problems will proliferate throughout the United States down to the smallest cities and towns.

Bibliography

Advancement Project, August 2006, *Gang Activity Reduction Strategy - Phase I Report*

Almonte, Paul. Street Gangs. Toronto, California: Crestwood House, 1994.

Alonso. Alejandro A., 2004, *Racialized Identities and the Formation of Black Gangs in Los Angeles*, Urban Geography, vol. 25, pp. 658-674.

Arthur, Richard. Gangs and Schools. Holmes Beach, FL: Learning Publications, 1992.

Baker, Phillip. Blood Posse. New York: St. Martin's Press, 1995.

Bensinger, Gad J. and Larigio, Arthur J. Gangs and Community Corrections. Chicago: Loyola University, 1992.

Brotherton David C. and Luis Barrios, 2004, The Almighty Latin King and Queen Nation: Street Politics and the Transformation of a New York City Gang, Columbia Press.

Bing, Lionel. Do or Die. New York: Harper Collins, 1994.

Canada, Geoffrey. Fish Stick Knife Gun. Boston, Mass.: Beacon Publishing Co., 1995.

Cantrell, Mary Lynn. Gang Identifiers and Terminology. Cantrell, Mary Lynn, The Journal of Emotional and Behavorial Problems, Vol. 1, (Spring 1992) 13-14.

Capozzoli, Thomas, and R. Steve McVey. Kids Killing Kids: Managing Violence and Gangs in Schools. Boca Raton, FL: St. Lucie Press, 2000.

Christensen, Loren. Skinhead Street Gangs. Boulder, Co: Paladin Press, 1994.

Conley, Catherine H. Street Gangs: Current Knowledge & Strategies. Lancaster, PA: Diane Publishing Company, 1994.

Dawley, David. A Nation of Lords: The Autobiography of the Vice Lords. Prospect Heights, Ill.: Waveland Press, Inc. 1992.

Devore, Cynthia DiLaura. Kids and Gangs. Edina, Minn.: Abdo & Daughters, 1994.

Doheny [Stacks] LB3013.3.C37 2000

Esbensen, F.-A., Osgood, D. W., Taylor, T. J., Peterson, D., & Freng, A., 2001, How great is G.R.E.A.T.?

Esbensen, F.-A., Peterson, D., Taylor, T. J., Freng, A., & Osgood, D. W. (2004). Gang prevention: A case study of a primary prevention program at the Long Grove, IL: Waveland Press, Inc.

Evans, Williams, Fitzgerald, Carla, Weigal, Dan & Sarah Chvilicek, 1999. Are Rural Gang Members Similar to their Urban

Counterparts? Implications for Rural Communities, *Youth & Society*, Vol. 30, 267-282.

Finn-Aage, Esbensen, 2000, Preventing Adolescent Gang Involvement, OJJDP Juvenile Justice Bulletin, U.S. Department of Justice, Washington D.C.

Finn-Aage, Esbensen & D. Wayne Odgood, 1999, Gang Resistance Education and Training (GREAT): Results From the National Evaluation, *Journal of Research in Crime and Delinquency*, Vol. 36, 194-225.

Fremon, Celeste, 2004, <u>G-Dog and the Homeboys: Father Greg Boyle and the Gangs of East Los Angeles.</u> University of New Mexico Press.

Fritsch, Eric J., Caeti, Tory J., & Robert W. Taylor, 1999, Gang Suppression through Saturation Patrol, Aggressive Curfew, and Truancy Enforcement: A Quasi-Experimental Test of the Dallas Anti-Gang Initiative, *Crime & Delinquency*, Vol. 45, 122-139.

Gang Manual, National Safety Training Institute, Santa Rosa, CA.

Gang Resource Guide. Sacramento: California District Attorneys Association, 1994.

Gang 2000: A Call to Action: the Attorney General's Report on the Impact of Criminal Street Gangs on Crime and Prevention by the Year 2000, California Department of Justice Division of Law Enforcement- Bureau of Investigation, March 1993.

Gangs in Correctional Facilities: A National Assessment. Laurel, Md.: American Correctional Association, 1993.

Gardner, Sandra. <u>Street Gangs in America.</u> New York: Franklin Watts, 1992.

Goldentyer, Debra. <u>Gangs.</u> Austin, TX: Raintree Steck Vaughn. 1994.

Hagedorn, J.M. <u>People and Folks: Gangs, Crime and the Underclass in a Rustbelt City.</u> Chicago: Lake View Press, 1988

Hasan H. A. 1998. Understanding the gang culture and how it relates to society and school. In: Park Hyun-Sook and Meyer Luanna et al. (Ed*) Making friends:The influences of culture and development.* Pp 263-283, Baltimore, MD: Paul H. Brookes.

Hayden, Tom, 2005, <u>Street Wars: Gangs and the Future of Violence.</u> New Press.

Hill, Karl G., Howell, James C. Howell, Hawkins, J. David, and Sara Battin-Pearson, 1999, Childhood Risk Factors for Adolescent Gang Membership: Results from Seattle, *Journal of Research in Crime and Delinquency*, vol. 36, pp 300-322.

Huff, Ronald C. and Arnold P. Goldstein, (eds.) <u>The Gang Intervention Handbook.</u> Champaign, IL: Research Press, 1993.

Huff, Ronald. C. (ed). <u>Gangs in America.</u> Newbury Park, Ca: Sage, 1990.

Huff, Ronald C., 1998, Comparing the Criminal Behavior of Youth
        Gangs and At-Risk Youth, National Institute of Justice, Washington
        D.C.

Jankowski, M.S. Islands in the Street: Gangs and American Urban
        Society. Berkeley: University Of California Press, 1995.

Justice Policy Institute, 2006. *Ganging Up On Communities: Putting
        Gang Crime in Context.*

Klein, Malcolm W. The American Street Gang: Its Nature, Prevalence,
        and Control. Carey, NC: Oxford University Press, 1995.

Klein, Malcolm, XaxonThe Modern Gang Reader, Malcolm W. Klein,
        Cheryl L. Xaxon, Jody Miller, Roxbury Publishing Company, Los
        Angeles, 1995.

Knox, Mike. Gangsta in the House. Troy, Michigan.: Momentum
        Books, 1995.

Korem, Daniel J. Streetwise Parents, Foolproof Kids. 2nd rev. ed.
        Richardson, TX: International Focus Press, 1995.
        Korem, Daniel J. Suburban Gangs---The Affluent Rebels.
        Richardson, TX: International Focus Press, 1994.

Landre, Rick, Mike Miller, and Dee Porter. Gangs: A Handbook for
        Community

Lane, Jodi & James W. Meeker, 2000, Subcultural Diversity and the Fear
        of Crime and Gangs, *Crime & Delinquency*, Vol. 46, 497-521

Levitt, Steven D. & Sudhir A. Venkatesh, 2000, An Economic Analysis
        of a Drug-Selling Gang's Finance, *The Quarterly Journal of
        Economics*, August, 755-789.

Maxon, Cheryl L. Street Gangs and Drug Sales in Two Suburban
        Communities. Washington, DC: National Institute of Justice, U.S.
        Department of Justice, 1995.

Maxson, Cheryl, 1998, Gangs on the Move, OJJDP Juvenile Justice
        Bulletin, Washington D.C.

Monti, Daniel J. Wannabe: Gangs in Suburbs and Schools. Cambridge,
        Mass.: Basil Blackwell, 1994.

Office of Justice and Delinquency Prevention, 2000, Youth Gangs,
        Programs and Strategies, U.S. Department of Justice, Washington
        D.C.

Office of Juvenile Justice and Delinquency Prevention. Gang
        Suppression and Intervention: Problems and Response. Research
        Summary, Washington, D.C.: 1994.

Oliver, Marilyn Tower. Gangs: Trouble in the Street. Springfield, N.J.:
        Enslow Publishers, 1995.

Olivero, M. J. Honor, Violence, and Upward Mobility: A Case Study of
        Chicago Gangs During the 1970's and 1980's. Edinburg, TX.
        University of Texas-Pan American Press, 1991.

Phillips, Susan A. <u>Wallbangin': Graffiti and Gangs in L.A.</u> Chicago IL: University of Chicago Press, 1999.

Rodrigues, Luis J. <u>Always Running -- La Vida Loca: Gang Days in L.A.</u> Willimantic. CO: Curbstone, 1993.

Rodriguez, Joseph, et al, 2000, <u>East Side Stories: Gang Life in East LA.</u> PowerHouse Books.

Ross, Jeffrey I. & Stephen C. Richards, 2002, <u>Behind Bars: Surviving Prison.</u> Alpha Books.

Sachs, Steven L. <u>Street Gang Awareness: A Resource Guide for Parents and Professionals.</u> Minneapolis, Minn.: Fairview Press, 1997.

Sanchez, Reymundo, 2001, <u>My Bloody Life: The Making of a Latin King.</u> Chicago Review Press.

Sanchez, Reymundo, 2004, <u>Once A King, Always A King: The Unmaking of a Latin King.</u> Chicago Review Press.

Sanders, W. B. <u>Gangbangs and Drive-Bys.</u> New York: Aldine, 1995

<u>School Violence in America's Cities.</u> Washington, DC: National League of Cities, 1994.

Scott Cummings and Daniel S. Monti (eds.). <u>Gangs.</u> Albany: State University of New York Press, 1993.

Shakur, Sanika. <u>Monster: The Autobiography of an L.A. Gang Member.</u> New York: Penguin, 1994.

Sides, Josh, 2004. Straight into Compton: American Dreams, Urban Nightmares, and the Metamorphosis of a Black Suburb. *American Quarterly*. -Vol. 56, No 3, pp. 583-605.

Sikes, Gini. 1997. <u>Eight Ball Chicks.</u> Anchor Press.

Sikes, Gina. <u>8 Ball Chicks.</u> New York: Doubleday, 1996.

Simpson, Colton, 2005, <u>Inside the Crips: Life inside L.A.'s Most Notorious Gang.</u> St. Martin's Press.

Spergel, Irving A., et al. <u>Gang Suppression and Intervention: An Assessment.</u> Washington, DC: Office of Juvenile Justice and Delinquency Prevention, U.S. Dept. of Justice, 1993.

Stark, Evan. <u>Everything You Wanted to Know About Street Gangs.</u> New York: Rosen Publishing, 1992.

Tita, George & Allan Abrahamse, 2004, *Gang Homicide in LA, 1981 - 2001*, California Attorney General's Office.

Tita, George, Scott Hiromoto, Jeremy Wilson, John Christian, & Clifford Grammich, 2004, *Gun Violence in the LAPD 77th Street Area*, Working Paper, Rand Public Safety and Justice

Urban Street Gang Enforcement. Alexandria, VA: Institute for Law and Justice, 1997.

Valentine. Bill. <u>Gang Intelligence Manual: Identifying and Understanding Modern Day</u>

Venkatesh, Sudhir Alladi, 2001 , Community Justice and the Gang: A Life-Course Perspective, Columbia University, New York: NY.

Violent Gangs in the United States. Boulder, Colorado. Paladin Press, 1995.
Virgil, James Diego. Barrio Gangs: Street Life and Identity in Southern California. Austin, TX. University
Vigil, James Diego, 2003, Rainbow of Gangs: Street Cultures in the Mega-City, Austin, TX. University
Webb, Margot. Coping with Street Gangs. New York: Harper Collins, 1994.
Wiener, Valerie. Winning the War against Youth Gangs: A Guide for Teens, Families, and Communities. Westport CT: Greenwood Press, 1999.
Williams, Stanley "Tookie", 1998, Life in Prison. Chronicle Books.
Williams, Stanley "Tookie", 2005, Blue Rage, Black Redemption. Damamli Publishing
Wright, Terrell, 2005, Home of the Body Bags. Venice:CA, Senegal Press.
Yablonsky, Lewis. 1997. Gangsters : Fifty Years of Madness, Drugs, and Death on the Streets of America . New York: New York Press.

Index